POLITICAL ARITHMETIC

NBER Series on Long-Term Factors in Economic Development
A National Bureau of Economic Research Series
Edited by Claudia Goldin

ALSO IN THE SERIES

Claudia Goldin
Understanding the Gender Gap: An Economic History of American Women (Oxford University Press, 1990)

Roderick Floud, Kenneth Wachter, and Annabel Gregory
Height, Health and History: Nutritional Status in the United Kingdom, 1750–1980 (Cambridge University Press, 1990)

Robert A. Margo
Race and Schooling in the South, 1880–1950: An Economic History (University of Chicago Press, 1990)

Samuel H. Preston and Michael R. Haines
Fatal Years: Child Mortality in Late Nineteenth-Century America (Princeton University Press, 1991)

Barry Eichengreen
Golden Fetters: The Gold Standard and the Great Depression, 1919–1939 (Oxford University Press, 1992)

Ronald N. Johnson and Gary D. Libecap
The Federal Civil Service System and the Problem of Bureaucracy: The Economics and Politics of Institutional Change (University of Chicago Press, 1994)

Naomi R. Lamoreaux
Insider Lending: Banks, Personal Connections, and Economic Development in Industrial New England (Cambridge University Press, 1994)

Lance E. Davis, Robert E. Gallman, and Karin Gleiter
In Pursuit of Leviathan: Technology, Institutions, Productivity, and Profits in American Whaling, 1816–1906 (University of Chicago Press, 1997)

Dora L. Costa
The Evolution of Retirement: An American Economic History, 1880–1990 (University of Chicago Press, 1998)

Joseph P. Ferrie
Yankeys Now: Immigrants in the Antebellum U.S., 1840–1860 (Oxford University Press, 1999)

Robert A. Margo
Wages and Labor Markets in the United States, 1820–1860 (University of Chicago Press, 2000)

Price V. Fishback and Shawn Everett Kantor
A Prelude to the Welfare State: The Origins of Workers' Compensation (University of Chicago Press, 2000)

Gerardo della Paolera and Alan M. Taylor
Straining at the Anchor: The Argentine Currency Board and the Search for Macroeconomic Stability, 1880–1935 (University of Chicago Press, 2001)

Werner Troesken
Water, Race, and Disease (MIT Press, 2004)

B. Zorina Khan
The Democratization of Invention: Patents and Copyrights in American Economic Development, 1790–1920 (Cambridge University Press, 2005)

Dora L. Costa and Matthew E. Kahn
Heroes and Cowards: The Social Face of War (Princeton University Press, 2008)

Roderick Floud, Robert W. Fogel, Bernard Harris, and Sok Chul Hong
The Changing Body: Health, Nutrition, and Human Development in the Western World since 1700 (Cambridge University Press, 2011)

Stanley L. Engerman and Kenneth L. Sokoloff
Economic Development in the Americas since 1500: Endowments and Institutions (Cambridge University Press, 2012)

Robert William Fogel, Enid M. Fogel, Mark Guglielmo, and Nathaniel Grotte
Political Arithmetic: Simon Kuznets and the Empirical Tradition in Economics (University of Chicago Press, 2013)

**Relation of the Directors to the Work and Publications
of the National Bureau of Economic Research**

1. The object of the NBER is to ascertain and present to the economics profession, and to the public more generally, important economic facts and their interpretation in a scientific manner without policy recommendations. The Board of Directors is charged with the responsibility of ensuring that the work of the NBER is carried on in strict conformity with this object.

2. The President shall establish an internal review process to ensure that book manuscripts proposed for publication DO NOT contain policy recommendations. This shall apply both to the proceedings of conferences and to manuscripts by a single author or by one or more co-authors but shall not apply to authors of comments at NBER conferences who are not NBER affiliates.

3. No book manuscript reporting research shall be published by the NBER until the President has sent to each member of the Board a notice that a manuscript is recommended for publication and that in the President's opinion it is suitable for publication in accordance with the above principles of the NBER. Such notification will include a table of contents and an abstract or summary of the manuscript's content, a list of contributors if applicable, and a response form for use by Directors who desire a copy of the manuscript for review. Each manuscript shall contain a summary drawing attention to the nature and treatment of the problem studied and the main conclusions reached.

4. No volume shall be published until forty-five days have elapsed from the above notification of intention to publish it. During this period a copy shall be sent to any Director requesting it, and if any Director objects to publication on the grounds that the manuscript contains policy recommendations, the objection will be presented to the author(s) or editor(s). In case of dispute, all members of the Board shall be notified, and the President shall appoint an ad hoc committee of the Board to decide the matter; thirty days additional shall be granted for this purpose.

5. The President shall present annually to the Board a report describing the internal manuscript review process, any objections made by Directors before publication or by anyone after publication, any disputes about such matters, and how they were handled.

6. Publications of the NBER issued for informational purposes concerning the work of the Bureau, or issued to inform the public of the activities at the Bureau, including but not limited to the NBER Digest and Reporter, shall be consistent with the object stated in paragraph 1. They shall contain a specific disclaimer noting that they have not passed through the review procedures required in this resolution. The Executive Committee of the Board is charged with the review of all such publications from time to time.

7. NBER working papers and manuscripts distributed on the Bureau's web site are not deemed to be publications for the purpose of this resolution, but they shall be consistent with the object stated in paragraph 1. Working papers shall contain a specific disclaimer noting that they have not passed through the review procedures required in this resolution. The NBER's web site shall contain a similar disclaimer. The President shall establish an internal review process to ensure that the working papers and the web site do not contain policy recommendations, and shall report annually to the Board on this process and any concerns raised in connection with it.

8. Unless otherwise determined by the Board or exempted by the terms of paragraphs 6 and 7, a copy of this resolution shall be printed in each NBER publication as described in paragraph 2 above.

POLITICAL ARITHMETIC

Simon Kuznets and the Empirical Tradition in Economics

ROBERT WILLIAM FOGEL, ENID M. FOGEL,
MARK GUGLIELMO, AND NATHANIEL GROTTE

The University of Chicago Press CHICAGO AND LONDON

Winner of the 1993 Nobel Prize for Economics, **Robert William Fogel** is the Charles R. Walgreen Distinguished Service Professor of American Institutions at the Booth School of Business, director of the Center for Population Economics, and a member of the Department of Economics and of the Committee on Social Thought at the University of Chicago. He is also a research associate of the National Bureau of Economic Research. **Enid M. Fogel** was associate dean of students at the Booth School of Business. **Mark Guglielmo** is assistant professor of economics at Bentley University. **Nathaniel Grotte** is associate director of the Center for Population Economics.

The University of Chicago Press, Chicago 60637
The University of Chicago Press, Ltd., London
© 2013 by The University of Chicago
All rights reserved. Published 2013.
Printed in the United States of America

22 21 20 19 18 17 16 15 14 13   1 2 3 4 5

ISBN-13: 978-0-226-25661-0 (cloth)
ISBN-13: 978-0-226-02072-3 (e-book)

Library of Congress Cataloging-in-Publication Data

Fogel, Robert William.
    Political arithmetic : Simon Kuznets and the empirical tradition in economics / Robert William Fogel, Enid M. Fogel, Mark Guglielmo, and Nathaniel Grotte.
        pages ; cm. — (NBER series on long-term factors in economic development)
    Includes bibliographical references and index.
    ISBN 978-0-226-25661-0 (cloth : alkaline paper) — ISBN 978-0-226-02072-3 (e-book) 1. Kuznets, Simon, 1901–1985—Influence. 2. Economics—Research—United States. 3. National income—United States—Accounting—History—20th century. 4. National Bureau of Economic Research. I. Fogel, Enid M. II. Guglielmo, Mark. III. Grotte, Nathaniel. IV. Title. V. Series: NBER series on long-term factors in economic development.
    HC110.I5F64 2013
    339.3'2—dc23

                                    2012031749

♾ This paper meets the requirements of ANSI/NISO Z39.48-1992 (Permanence of Paper).

Contents

To Penelope Enid Anderegg and Maximillian Thor Pietraszewski,
great-grandchildren of Enid and Bob

Preface

This book is about the scientific work of Simon Kuznets and his impact on economics as a discipline. Kuznets was the winner of the third Nobel Prize in economics, which he received in 1971 for his work on comparative economic growth. He was also an exceptionally inspiring teacher who influenced the research and teaching of some of the best economists in economics and demography.

The book begins with a view of the great accomplishments of the twentieth century. Chapter 1 offers a history of the development of economics as an academic discipline prior to World War I. Chapter 2 describes the establishment of the NBER as an objective collector and analyzer of economic data that would be useful to policymakers. Chapter 3 describes the development of national income accounting at the NBER as a major tool for analyzing and assessing the performance of the economy and for guiding government interventions. It also describes the leading role played by Kuznets in demonstrating the power of this tool as a successful guide to the allocation of available resources between military needs and the civilian economy during World War II. Chapter 4 deals with Kuznets's use of national income accounting to analyze the factors accounting for the differences in the rate of growth among nations, the specific work for which he was awarded the Nobel Prize. Chapter 5 reviews Kuznets's scientific methods. Chapter 6 examines the continuing impact of Kuznets's research and his influence on economics. Chapter 7 considers the global economy in the quarter century after Kuznets's death with forecasts of the nature and future of both the domestic and the global economies.

Kuznets is introduced early in the introduction, then recedes into the background until chapter 3. To lighten that drought, we address now a question often put to us: What was Kuznets like as a person? To Robert Fogel, he was a beloved teacher who took a fatherly interest in both the intellectual and the personal aspects of his students' lives. That interest did not end after those students completed their graduate work and were off teaching somewhere on their own. Kuznets encouraged them to keep in touch and come visit him at home whenever they were in town.

"And so we did," said Fogel. Enid and Bob, with children in tow, often visited Simon either at his office or his home. After bouncing each of the boys on his knee and talking with them for a bit, he would settle back in his chair and ask, "So, Mr. Fogel, what have you been working on lately?" He listened to the answer carefully, sometimes probing for more detail, occasionally offering suggestions.

Kuznets had many students, all of whom wanted his help after they were launched on their own careers. When Fogel asked Simon to give a paper at his workshop in Chicago, Simon said, "You don't need me." But, when a less successful student issued the same invitation, Kuznets accepted without hesitation.

One day shortly after Simon's death, Fogel was at Kuznets's home, helping organize his papers for deposit at the Harvard Library. "Simon," his widow, Edith, said, "was modestly immodest." By that, she meant he was immodest in his desire to identify and measure the driving forces of economic growth but modest about his capacity to do so. He was always more focused on what he still had to learn than on what he already knew.

Born in Pinsk, Russia, on April 30, 1901, Kuznets received his education in primary school and gymnasium in Kharkov. He served briefly as a section head in the bureau of labor statistics of the Ukraine before emigrating to the United States in 1922. He entered Columbia University, where he received his B.A. in 1923, his M.A. in 1924, and his Ph.D. in 1926. His principal teacher at Columbia, and his lifelong mentor, was Wesley Clair Mitchell, a founder of the NBER and its director of research from 1920 to 1946.

Kuznets was a member of the research staff of the NBER from 1927 to 1961. It is there that he met Edith Handler. They were married in

1929 and had two children, Paul and Judith. Kuznets also held professional appointments in economics and statistics at the University of Pennsylvania (1930–54) and in economics at Johns Hopkins University (1954–60) and Harvard University (1960–71). During 1932–34, he served in the Department of Commerce, where he constructed the first official estimates of U.S. national income and laid the basis for the National Income Section. During World War II, he served as the associate director of the Bureau of Planning and Statistics of the War Production Board. He was instrumental in establishing the Conference on Research in Income and Wealth (which brought together government officials and academic economists engaged in the development of the U.S. national income and product accounts) in 1936 and helped establish its international counterpart, the International Association for Research in Income and Wealth, in 1947. He served as an adviser to the governments of China, Japan, India, Korea, Taiwan, and Israel in the establishment of their national systems of economic information.

Despite his extensive activities in the design of government programs of economic intelligence and his work in consulting with such private agencies as the Growth Center of Yale University and the Social Science Research Council, Kuznets was a prolific analyst of economic processes and institutions. During the course of his career, he produced thirty-one books and over two hundred papers, many of which set off major new streams of research. Among the fields in which he pioneered, in addition to national income accounting, were the study of seasonal, cyclic, and secular fluctuations in economic activity; the impact of population change on economic activity; the study of the nature and causes of modem economic growth based on the measurement of national aggregate statistics; the household distribution of income and its trends in the United States and other countries; the measurement and analysis of the role of capital in economic growth; the impact of ideology and other institutional factors on economic growth; changing patterns in consumption and in the use of time; and methods of economic and statistical analysis. Kuznets's intellectual contributions were acknowledged by his colleagues in many ways, including his election as president of the American Statistical Association in 1949 and of the American Economic Association in 1954.

Introduction: The Amazing Twentieth Century

The human race (*Homo sapiens*) is about 200,000 years old. Measured in generations of 30 years, that translates into about sixty-seven hundred generations. In all but the last four hundred generations, our ancestors were hunters and gatherers with little ability to alter their environments.

During the last four hundred generations, we discovered agriculture and developed it to the point that it became the principal source of our food supply and provided a diet far better than previously experienced by the human race.

In 1800 (seven generations ago), it took five people working on farms in America and Western Europe to support one person working off the farm. Today, one person working on an American farm feeds three hundred people. In the short time span of two hundred years, farmers have declined from over 80 percent of the American labor force to less than 2 percent.

It was not until four generations ago that the majority of the labor force in the United States became nonagricultural. During the last four generations, there was a remarkable improvement in health, labor capacity, and longevity. During the twentieth century, life expectancy at birth increased by about thirty-five years in the rich nations, going from about forty-four to about seventy-nine years. Thus, in three of the last four generations, there has been a larger increase in life expectancy than in the whole previous history of *Homo sapiens*.

Not only has the length of life increased remarkably since 1900, but also the age of onset of disabilities has been pushed back by more than ten years. Moreover, the share of the aged population that becomes severely disabled has dropped from 80 percent to less than 40 percent. Rapid advances in biomedical technology since the late 1930s made it possible to sharply mitigate (sometimes even to reverse) the disabilities at advanced ages and dramatically improve the quality of life.

It is likely that the median age of death (the age by which half of a birth cohort has died) will increase from 78 years for the birth cohort of the 1920s to about 105 years for the current cohort of undergraduate college students, an increase of 27 years in just three generations.

Until recently, we were limited to learning about mankind through the study of bone fragments and other ancient artifacts carried out by archaeologists. With the advent of modern analytic tools and techniques, we have been able to develop and model rich insights into how we, as a people, live our lives amid a range of varied and rich economic choices.

During the 1920s and early 1930s, economists at the NBER developed measures of the national output of goods and services and helped establish a permanent bureau in the Department of Commerce to oversee the work of this measurement. Simon Kuznets was the overarching leader of this enterprise, which resulted in the estimation of the now-familiar statistics GNP and GNP per capita. These statistics, originally estimated by month and year from the late 1920s, were eventually pushed back to 1800 and carried forward to the present. They are derived from a complex set of accounts now regularly created by the federal government called *national income and product accounts*.

In this complex array of accounts, the output of the economy is measured in three ways, with each way revealing something different about the operation of the economy:

1.   The *value-added* or *production approach* reveals how much each industry adds to GNP.
2.   The *income approach* reveals how much each factor of production (labor, land, and capital) contributes to GNP.

3.   The *expenditure approach* reveals how the consumption of GNP
     was divided among household consumption, business invest-
     ment, government expenditures, and net exports.

Kuznets did not work out the full array of national income and product accounts, but he initiated the process and gave it a powerful impetus that persuaded economists and government leaders that it was an
indispensable tool in the management of the economy.

Although the GNP estimates were a huge advance in the statistical
arsenal of economists, they are no longer adequate. They do not take
into account *technophysio evolution*, by which we mean the synergism
between rapid technological change and the improvement in human
physiology. Because of this synergism, human beings have acquired
so great a degree of control over their environment that they are set
apart not only from all other species but also from all previous generations of *Homo sapiens*. This new degree of control has enabled our
species to increase its average body size by over 50 percent, to increase
its average longevity by more than 100 percent, and to greatly improve
the robustness and capacity of its vital organ systems.

Worldwide, the most important aspect of technophysio evolution
is the continuing conquest of chronic malnutrition, which was almost
universal three centuries ago. At the beginning of the eighteenth century, such countries as France and Great Britain could not produce
enough food to keep more than 80 percent of the potential labor force
regularly employed. Moreover, those who were in the labor force had
on average only about a quarter of the daily energy that is currently
available for work. Today, by contrast, food is so abundant that obesity is a significant problem.

The improvement in nutrition and human physiology accounts for
much of the economic growth of rich nations. It has, for example,
recently been estimated that about half of British economic growth
since 1790 was due to technophysio evolution.[1] Much of this gain
came from improvements in human thermodynamic efficiency. The

---

1. For a more extensive discussion of technophysio evolution, see Floud, Fogel, Harris, and
Hong (2011).

rate of converting human energy input into work output appears to have increased by about 50 percent over the past seven generations.

One aspect of technophysio evolution has been a change in the structure of consumption and in the division of discretionary time between work and leisure. Sleep, meals, and essential hygiene, which are biologically determined, required about ten hours of the day a century ago, as they do today. The remaining fourteen hours represent discretionary time. A century ago, most of the discretionary time of the typical head of a household in Western Europe and America was devoted to earning a living. He worked about thirty-one hundred hours a year in the marketplace to provide for the family, and he also had unpaid chores at home, as well as travel to and from work, that occupied another eleven hundred hours. Only a minuscule amount of time was left for leisure each day.

Over the course of the twentieth century, annual hours of work have fallen by nearly half, so much so that the household head in a rich country now usually works only about seventeen hundred hours per year in the marketplace. Indeed, on the average day, he spends more hours at leisure than at work. Because of the mechanization of the household, the typical married woman also spends more time at leisure than at work.

Leisure is not a synonym for indolence but a reference to desirable forms of effort or work. As the Irish playwright George Bernard Shaw put it in *The Intelligent Woman's Guide to Socialism and Capitalism* (1928), "Labor is doing what we must; leisure is doing what we like; and rest is doing nothing whilst our bodies and minds are recovering from their fatigue." In order to avoid confusion, *work* refers to an activity that requires energy over and above the basal metabolic rate. Activity aimed primarily at earning a living is *earnwork*. Purely voluntary activity, even if it incidentally carries some payment with it, is *volwork*.

Why have hours of earnwork declined so much in recent years? The answer to that question is suggested by the fact that it is not just daily and weekly hours of earnwork that have declined. The share of lifetime discretionary hours spent in earnwork has declined even more rapidly, partly because the average age of entering the labor force is five years later than it used to be, and partly because the average period of retirement is about eleven years longer than it was a century ago.

Today, people are willing to forgo earnwork, even though the extra hours would allow them to buy more things, because they are approaching saturation not only in food and other necessities but also in a whole array of consumer durables. Because of rapid technological change, goods that during the first third of the twentieth century used to be thought of as luxuries or were only dreams or science fiction are now available even to the poor. A century ago, the typical household head had to labor 1,800 hours to acquire the family's annual food supply. But, by the end of the twentieth century, that task required just 260 hours. All in all, commodities that used to account for over 80 percent of household consumption could be obtained in greater abundance than previously, with less than a third of either the market or the household labor once required.

As a result, there have been enormous changes in the pattern of national expenditures, especially when the extra hours of leisure are valued at what workers could have earned if they remained at work. Food, clothing, and shelter, which used to account for three-quarters of consumption, now account for just 12 percent. On the other hand, leisure has risen from 18 percent of consumption to 67 percent. There has also been a vast increase in expenditures for health care and for education.

However, the computations presented so far are inadequate to portray the full extent of economic growth over the past century because they do not take into account improvements in the quality of output, especially in such services as education and health care. Children in high schools are taught more today than postgraduate college students used to be taught a generation ago, let alone two generations ago. Adolescent children today know more about computers than most of their parents do.

Even more dramatic are the improvements in health care. A century and a half ago, people in their forties were more afflicted by chronic disabilities than people in their late fifties and early sixties are today. Not only has the average age of onset of disabilities been delayed by ten or so years, but, once those disabilities appear, there are also now numerous effective interventions. Hernias, which used to be permanent and exceedingly painful conditions, afflicting one of every four males, can now be repaired by a surgical procedure that in the United States requires hospitalization for only twenty-three hours. Other areas where medical interventions have been highly effective include genitourinary conditions, control of hypertension and reduction in the incidence of stroke, replacement of knee and hip joints, curing of cataracts, and chemotherapies that reduce the incidence of osteoporosis and heart disease.

Yet most of these great advances in health care and education are overlooked in accounts of GNP because of the difficulty in measuring them. The inadequacy of the national income and product accounts in dealing with these issues was recognized by Kuznets, who sketched the probable magnitude of the error. The problem stems from the fact that production of health care and education is measured by inputs instead of by output. An hour of a doctor's time is considered no more effective today than an hour of a doctor's time was three-quarters of a century ago, before the age of antibiotics and modern surgery. It has recently been estimated that, if properly measured, improvements in health care would add significantly to the level of per capita income, but such calculations have not yet made their way into the GNP accounts. In the case of the United States, rough estimates indicate that allowance for such factors as the increase in leisure time, the improvement in the quality of health care, and the improvements in the quality of education would come close to doubling the U.S. annual growth rate over the past century (from 1.8 to more than 3 percent per annum).

What is the implication of these statistics for the understanding of change in standards of living for the typical American? If we use the conventional measure of growth, the real income of the typical American in 2000 was six times greater than it was in 1900. However, if the adjusted measure is used, Americans in 2000 had real incomes that were twenty times greater than they were in 1900. In other words, 70 percent of the goods and services that Americans enjoyed at the end of the twentieth century were outside the measured economy.

We now want to consider briefly another aspect of the changing nature of economic growth. That is the impact of high levels of economic attainment on the distribution of the output of the economy and households. Those who worry about egalitarian issues tend to think about distribution in terms of material goods, such as food, clothing, and shelter, which used to constitute over 80 percent of the consumption of households. To be poor in the decades before World War I was to be deprived of these tangible essentials of life and to be vulnerable to disease and early death. In that era, things that you could see, count, weigh, or otherwise directly measure constituted the overwhelming output of an economy.

During the last six or so decades of the twentieth century, the domination of output by material products began to be eroded at an increasing rate. The rise to dominance of immaterial commodities is symbolized by the growth of such professional occupations as physicians, mathematicians, natural scientists, lawyers, teachers, and engineers from barely 4 percent of the labor force in 1900 to over a third today. Similarly, the main form of capital at the end of the twentieth century was not buildings, machines, or electrical grids but labor skills, what economists call *human capital* or *knowledge capital*. Both for individuals and for businesses, it is the size and quality of these immaterial assets that determine success in competitive markets and in conditions of life for ordinary people.

The agenda for egalitarian policies that has dominated reform movements for most of the past century, the modernist agenda, was based on material redistribution. The critical aspect of a *postmodern* egalitarian agenda is not the distribution of money income, or food, or shelter, or consumer durables. Although there are still glaring inadequacies in the distribution of material commodities, the most intractable maldistributions in rich countries such as the United States are in the realm of spiritual or immaterial assets. These are the critical assets in the struggle for self-realization.

Some proponents of egalitarianism insist on characterizing the *material* level of the poor today as being harsh. They confound current and past conditions of living. Failure to recognize the enormous *material* gains over the last century, even for the poor, impedes rather than advances the struggle against chronic poverty in rich nations, whose principal characteristic is the *spiritual estrangement* from the mainstream society of those so afflicted. Although material assistance is an important element in the struggle to overcome spiritual estrangement, such assistance will not be properly targeted if one assumes that improvement in material conditions naturally leads to spiritual improvement.

Realization of the potential of an individual is not something that can be legislated by the state, nor can it be provided to the weak by the strong. The government cannot transfer virtue from those who have it in abundance to those who are bereft of it. Nor can the rich write out checks denominated in virtue. Self-realization has to develop within each individual on the basis of a succession of choices. The emphasis on individual choice does not mean that other individuals and institutions play no role. Quite the contrary, the quality of the choices and the range of opportunities depend critically on how well endowed an individual is with critical spiritual resources.

The quest for spiritual equity thus turns not so much on money as on access to immaterial assets, most of which are transferred and developed privately rather than through the market. Moreover, some of the most critical spiritual assets, such as a sense of purpose, self-esteem, a sense of discipline, a vision of opportunity, and a thirst for knowledge, are transferred at very young ages.

Although there are spiritually deprived individuals at all ages, the two main concentrations are among the alienated young and the elderly. Some of the young are children in single-parent families whose mothers are themselves spiritually deprived and hence incapable of transferring vital spiritual assets. The other large group is concentrated among the elderly. In the United States, one-third of those over age sixty-five suffer from depression because they are cut off from normal social networks.

Solving these severe problems of social and economic estrangement requires a variety of new educational programs and systems of mentoring the needy. These programs cannot be achieved by the government alone or even primarily but involve mobilizing a vast reservoir of individuals with spiritual abundance who are prepared to assist.

A third way in which economic growth is changing is in the rapid and radical shift in the locus of global markets for durables and high-tech services. The observation is hardly new. Thousands of articles have been written during the past decade on the emerging markets of Southeast Asia. Nevertheless, the full meaning of this development for the unfolding of global economic growth during the next generation is still poorly understood.

1 : : The Rise of Academic Economists before World War I

Academic economists are so prominent in the making and execution of economic policy that it is easy to take their role in the operation of the modern welfare state for granted. However much of a compliment such acceptance might appear to be, it slights the role of economists as contributors to the creation of the welfare state and as a group of professionals who generated public demand for their expertise. The rise of academic economists to their current prominence in public life did not happen overnight. We begin by describing some aspects of the evolution of the economics profession in the United States and the large role played by academic economists in the design and triumph of the welfare state.

Academic economists had little impact on the economic policies of federal and state governments during the first three-quarters of the nineteenth century. This absence of influence is not explained merely by the prevalence of laissez-faire doctrine. Nor is it explained by the lack of involvement of government in economic matters or the lack of instruments through which federal and state governments might have intervened in economic affairs. Quite the contrary, economic policy was central to politics throughout the nineteenth century. Among the issues debated and acted on were tariffs; taxes on property, sales, and income; banking policy; the promotion of internal improvements (roads, railroads, and waterways); government action to ameliorate business cycles; reduction of the labor supply through control of immigration; pensions for veterans; land distribution; the subsidization of education; and unemployment compensation, workers' compensation, gender differences in pay and occupations, and other aspects of the alleviation of poverty.

By and large, the theorists of and experts on these issues before the Civil War were not academics but politicians, merchants, bankers, planters, journalists, artisans, and theologians, some of whom had little or no college education. This is not to say that academic economists did not sometimes write books and articles or collect and analyze statistical data. In 1843, George Tucker, a professor of moral philosophy at the University of Virginia, published an estimate of U.S. national income based on the decennial census of 1840 (see Tucker 1843).[1] A prophet of industrialization and population growth, Tucker was involved in politics and served a term in the House of Representatives. The academy also produced a few writers of textbooks on economics. The most widely used text during the three decades before the Civil War, *The Elements of Political Economy* (1837), was written by the Reverend Francis Wayland, the president of Brown University, a principal leader of the Northern Baptist Church, and an advocate of laissez-faire. Its objective, Wayland wrote, was to set forth God's laws, so far discovered, regarding the production and distribution of those products that constitute the wealth of a nation (Dorfman 1946; Studenski 1958).

Property, Wayland argued, was founded on the "will of God," and it was acquired directly as his immediate gift (as with land) or by labor. As for labor, Wayland accepted the general validity of the Malthusian doctrine that the excessive fertility of laborers tended to increase their numbers and reduce their wages to the point of starvation and death. But that tendency was kept in abeyance in the United States because capital increased faster than the population. Hence, distressing poverty was rare except when precipitated by intemperance, indolence, and similar vices. The favorable demand for labor and the lagging supply made it possible for industrious workers to accumulate capital in a relatively short period of time. It followed that combinations

1. Tucker is also well-known as the author of a pamphlet arguing for the freeing of slaves (see Tucker 1801).

of labor (i.e., unions) were not only counterproductive to the interest of labor but also unjust because they deprived laborers of the right to dispose of their labor and, as with legislative interference, they were destructive of industry.

The Response to Industrial Concentration

The widespread embrace of laissez-faire before the Civil War was promoted by an economy that consisted of small producing units. Both rural and urban laborers could believe that by hard work and frugality they would become the masters of their own businesses. After the Civil War, however, new technologies promoted such large economies of scale that many small operations were driven out of competition in one industry after another, including iron and steel, petroleum, meatpacking, milling, chemicals, and banking. Large-scale enterprises arose not only because new inventions required massive investments in plants (as in Bessemer steel) or in grids (as in electricity). They were also promoted by the enormous expansion of urban markets and technologies that drastically reduced the cost of transportation and communication. As a result, efficient firms could compete in distant markets in which inefficient local producers had previously been protected by the natural barriers of high transportation and distribution costs.

The losers in this competitive struggle did not accept their fate stoically but appealed to the government for legislation that would offset their technological disadvantages. Small millers in upstate New York demanded reductions in their freight rates to make them more competitive with large-scale millers in Milwaukee. Small banks that charged higher interest rates in their local markets demanded protection from the eastern banks that began offering comparable services at lower rates. Small refineries called on legislators to prevent Standard Oil from undercutting their markets with what they described as *predatory pricing*. Farmers in Iowa condemned the railroads for charging more to ship a ton of wheat two hundred miles to Chicago than it cost to ship that same ton nine hundred miles from Chicago to New York City.

Thus, the last quarter of the nineteenth century and the first quarter of the twentieth witnessed a fierce confrontation between the new big businesses and traditional businesses. On the one side were multimillionaires, the "robber barons." On the other were small rural and urban businesses, farmers, and those who labored for the robber barons.

Railroads were the earliest and the most persistent target. During the railroad-building booms preceding and following the Civil War, state and local governments outdid each other in offering tax exemptions and other inducements for companies to lay track through their areas. Once the railroads were completed, however, discontent arose with the structure of rates, the quality of service, and the failure of railroads to pay their fair share of taxes. Led by the principal farmers' organization in the Midwest, the Grange, lobbies were successful in passing state laws regulating the railroads, in raising taxes on railroad properties, and in bringing suits in the courts.[2]

Labor also protested, often using its most powerful weapon, the strike. During the Civil War, the first of the great railroad brotherhoods was organized among locomotive engineers, and that example was followed by other groups of workers on and off the railroad. By 1870, there were thirty-two national trade unions, and most of the larger cities had also established trade assemblies and publications. The most violent strike of the postwar era began during July 1877 in response to wage cuts on many of the railroads east of the Mississippi. Trains were halted by workers, and troops were brought out to deal with angry mobs. Buildings were burned and blood spilled in Baltimore, Pittsburgh, and other major railroad centers. By the time the strike was over, about one hundred people had been killed, and the resulting property damage ran into the millions of dollars. The conflict was so bloody it revived fears that America could be visited by a revolution of the French type. Those fears were reawakened in 1892 and again in 1893 when strikes at the giant Carnegie Steel Company and the Pullman Palace Car Company touched off pitched battles and

2. For this and the three preceding paragraphs, see Benson (1955), Hughes (1991), Lebergott (1964), and Temin (1964).

mob violence, and state militias and federal troops had to be brought in to reestablish order. Labor strife led some reformers to doubt the prevailing theories of poverty and to question whether the frontier was still an adequate safety valve for urban labor (Fogel 2000).

The Social Gospel Movement and the Wisconsin Idea

The change in thought is illustrated by the career of the Reverend John Bascom, who taught economics at Williams College and published a textbook in political economy in 1859. Holding views quite similar to those of Wayland, Bascom argued that the tactics of trade unions, especially strikes, were vicious attempts by incompetent workers to prevent workers with "superior intelligence, economy, and integrity" from achieving the benefits of free competition. By the mid-1880s, however, when Bascom was serving as the fifth president of the University of Wisconsin, he deplored the prevailing lack of sympathy for trade unions. Capital, he charged, was combining in ways that made the contest between capital and labor highly unequal. Consequently, government should curb the tyranny of big business and favor labor more. The state, he believed, had to become a vehicle for social improvement, including a mild redistribution of income from the rich to the poor (Dorfman 1946, 967 [quote]; Curti and Carstensen 1949; Henderson 1993).

Bascom was one of the pioneers of the new reform movement that historians refer to as the "Social Gospel." Although his change of economic heart was typical of many of the leaders of this wave of reform, it would be a mistake to presume that the evolution reflected a change in underlying spirit, from complacency to compassion. The reformers of the "Second Great Awakening," the name that historians have given to the reform movement that began during the antebellum era, could hardly be called *complacent*. They were imbued with the ethic of benevolence. Their ambition was to make the world "a fit place for the imminent return of Christ." They were committed to the "universal reformation of the world" and to the "complete and final overthrow" of "war, slavery, licentiousness, and all such evils and abominations." But they were slow in recognizing a new set of issues precipitated by the rise of big business (McLoughlin 1978, 128 [quotes]; Fogel 2000; Curti and Carstensen 1949; Henderson 1993).

Although the Social Gospel movement arose out of the theological currents of the Second Great Awakening, it was transformed by the deepening economic and social strife of the 1870s and 1880s, by the intensification of corruption in the rapidly growing cities, and by the intellectual turmoil precipitated by the new findings in geology and by the Darwinian controversy. In this context, Social Gospel leaders argued that, if America were to revitalize itself, it would have to change not only its creed, its theory of man's relationship to God, but also its ethics. It would have to make poverty not a personal failure but a failure of society, and evil would have to be seen not as a personal sin but as a sin of society. According to these radicals, it was the obligation of the state to improve the economic condition of the poor by favoring labor and redistributing income, reforms necessary to put an end to urban corruption (Fogel 2000; Curti and Carstensen 1949; Henderson 1993).

Bascom was not only one of the earliest academic expositors of Social Gospel theory; he was also a highly influential teacher who put an indelible stamp on the culture of the University of Wisconsin and, in time, on the state government of Wisconsin. Bascom's influence at the university was intensified and extended after 1891 by Richard T. Ely, the most prominent economist of the period and the most ardent academic expositor of Social Gospel theory. Hired to head the new School of Economics, Political Science and History, Ely sought to create a program that would do for the civil service what West Point had done for engineering. He quickly hired two of his former students from Johns Hopkins University and developed a large number of courses on such topics as the history of political economy, recent economic theories, statistics, money, and the distribution of wealth (Henderson 1993; Furner 1990; Curti and Carstensen 1949).

Three events made it possible for Ely to pursue his vision of academics as partners with politicians in the creation of a welfare state. The first was the election of Robert M. LaFollette, a disciple of Bascom's, as governor of Wisconsin in 1900. The second was the accession of Charles R. Van Hise, another disciple of Bascom's and a classmate of

LaFollette's, as university president in 1903. The third was the arrival of John R. Commons, a student of Ely's at Johns Hopkins and a zealous Social Gospeler, as professor of economics in 1904. Commons, who had had a good deal of experience with government and business, had learned that it was necessary to tone down the religious rhetoric. He also emphasized that his arguments for reform were aimed not at undermining capitalism but at regulating the abuses of big businesses. Commons recognized that the case for change had to be based on careful empirical analysis of the organization of business and the operation of labor markets. This approach became known as *institutional economics* (Henderson 1993; Furner 1990; Curti and Carstensen 1949).

When LaFollette needed advice on the implementation of his legislative agenda, he turned to Commons. Commons drafted legislation for a civil service bill (which based employment on competitive examinations) and for a bill establishing a Wisconsin state commission to regulate railroads, both of which were enacted in 1905. He was subsequently involved in designing the state's programs for regulating public utilities, workmen's compensation, and apprenticeships. Other university economists who were involved either in consulting with the government or in serving on regulatory commissions included Thomas S. Adams (a specialist in public finance and taxation) and Balthasar H. Meyer (a specialist in railroad regulations). Beyond economics, members of the faculty were drawn to serve on state commissions from such diverse fields as geology, bacteriology, agronomy, and engineering. In 1908, about one-sixth of the university faculty had appointments on government commissions (Henderson 1993; Furner 1990; Curti and Carstensen 1949).

The "Wisconsin Idea," as LaFollette called it, for a partnership between academic and political reformers was duplicated in other states. At local and state levels of government, where constitutional scruples against government intervention in the economy were relatively weak, many politicians saw the advantages of using nonpartisan academic experts to investigate the issues reflecting popular discontent, while academic reformers, such as Ely and Commons, believing that the facts were on their side, saw such investigations as powerful instruments in rallying public and legislative support for proposals they embraced. Of course, belief in the efficacy of particular policies need not undermine fruitful, objective research, as the career of Commons illustrates. Everything depends on the investigator's turn of mind, on his or her dedication to professional standards.

The Entry of Economists into the Making of Federal Policy

The idea of a partnership between academic and political reformers that was so strong in Wisconsin was not easily transferred to the federal level. Although other universities had religiously driven economists who wanted to turn the federal government into a welfare state, the majority of economists outside Wisconsin were orthodox in their economic principles. They believed that, although there was a legitimate role for government to play in addressing market failures, that role had to be lightly exercised. Otherwise, the government might become a serious obstacle to the effective performance of the economy. Another and perhaps more formidable barrier to the penetration of the federal government was the absence of a strong demand for economists among members of Congress and officials in the executive branch. Prior to World War I, the demand for the advice of economists in the making of federal policy was as modest as the supply of economists who sought to influence federal policy directly.

Nevertheless, between 1880 and World War I, economists did become increasingly involved in federal policymaking. Three factors drove this evolutionary process. The first was the rising tide of unrest over economic conditions among workers, farmers, and small businessmen, particularly the periodic outbreaks of violence by railroad and industrial workers. These outbreaks stirred alarm in Congress, which took measures to obtain more information about real wages and other aspects of the economy. The second factor was the emergence of a small corps of economists with expertise on the issues of concern to Congress and the president. As late as 1900, there were hardly seventy economists in the twenty-two top research universities of the nation. Some of these experts were largely self-taught, without doctorates in economics. This was, for example, true of Charles F.

Dunbar, the first person appointed to a chair in economics at Harvard, whose only earned degree was an A.B., awarded in 1851 (Parrish 1967). The third factor, especially after 1900, was the determined effort of Social Gospel economists to project their program for the transformation of the federal government into a welfare state. Fewer in number than mainstream, orthodox economists, the Social Gospelers were able to gain an audience in Congress and among other opinionmakers, partly because of their considerable expository skills, and partly because of the large role they played in amassing empirical evidence on the wretched conditions of life among a large proportion of industrial workers.

An important step in the transformation of the federal government into a welfare state was the establishment of an agency to systematically collect information on labor conditions. The U.S. Bureau of Labor Statistics (BLS) was established in 1885 with Carroll D. Wright, one of the self-taught economists and statisticians, as its first commissioner, a post he held until 1904. Although Wright (who taught at Johns Hopkins, Columbia, and Harvard Universities) was much closer in his economic analyses to such orthodox economists than he was to Ely, he believed that the rise of big business and the growth of an industrial labor force had produced injustices that required illumination. He had earlier pioneered the collection of data on the earnings and expenditures of working-class families and was one of the propounders of the so-called Engel curve, which purported to show, from cross-sectional data, how consumption of various items changed with income (Stigler 1954; Furner 1990). Although many of the projects undertaken by the BLS were dictated by requests for information by Congress, Wright launched many studies on his own initiative.

Data on changes in wages and prices for the entire period 1840–91 were collected at the request of the Senate Finance Committee, headed by Nelson Aldrich of Rhode Island. Using data obtained directly from the payrolls of eighty-eight companies and covering various occupations in twenty-one industries, the BLS was able to chart the progress of nominal wages. It also obtained data on the wholesale prices of two hundred articles going back to 1860 and of retail prices for a more limited period. These raw figures were converted into wage and price indices, initiating an important new statistical procedure. Out of this research was developed the first cost-of-living index, with weights obtained from a study of the household budgets of 2,561 working-class families (Furner 1990; Aldrich 1892, 1893).

The BLS also launched studies of wages and living standards in key industries and investigated the changing structure of the labor force, focusing on the problems of such groups as women, children, blacks, and railroad labor. Wright, who supported the development of craft trade unions, conducted surveys on labor laws in European countries, outlining existing and incipient entitlement programs, including workmen's compensation. Domestically, the BLS collected statistics on the impact of unions on wages and surveyed the annual number of strikes and lockouts. Such studies suggested, in one historian's assessment, "that unions exercised a restraining influence during depressions and actually helped to stabilize disorganized industries. . . . The BLS made no direct effort to assess the impact of strikes on distributive equity, but consistently implied that organized action was necessary to achieve a just division, and that aggressive wage demands supported necessary consumption" (Furner 1990, 252).

Economists were also drawn into the making of federal policy through the increasing number of commissions established by Congress to investigate pressing policy issues. The U.S. Industrial Commission (USIC), which operated between 1898 and 1902, was the first government agency to bring together a staff of trained economists in the federal government. Responding to the complaints of the Populists, leaders of small businesses, and labor, this commission investigated such issues as the impact of immigration on wages, the pricing policies of railroads, and industrial concentration. Edward Dana Durand of Cornell and Stanford Universities, who served as secretary of the commission, hired a number of young economists—including John R. Commons, Emory R. Johnson of the Wharton School at the University of Pennsylvania, and William Z. Ripley of the Massachusetts Institute of Technology—who would later gain national stature. The commission produced nineteen volumes of reports and testimony that influenced subsequent antitrust policies and legislation on immigration. The empirical evidence collected by the USIC and the analysis of the data were on a high level. On the whole, the reports recommended negotiations between unions and trusts as the best way to stabilize labor markets, ensure high levels of economic activity, and provide relatively high wages (Furner 1990).

Other congressional commissions that involved economists and that had a significant impact on economic policy included the Commission on Industrial Relations (CIR), which operated between 1913 and 1916, the National Monetary Commission (NMC) of 1908–12, and the U.S. Immigration Commission of 1909–15. Each of these was a response to political unrest touched off by business cycles. The findings of each commission provided the foundation for subsequent legislation. The Federal Reserve Act of 1913, for example, which established the Federal Reserve System, closely followed the recommendations of the NMC. Similarly, the forty-one-volume report of the Immigration Commission laid the basis for legislation enacted in the early 1920s ending unrestricted immigration and establishing quotas aimed at sharply limiting the entry into the United States of immigrants from Southern and Eastern Europe (Hughes 1991; Dorfman 1959a).

The papers and reports that did the most to promote the welfare state were those emanating from the CIR. With a research staff of fifty, mostly economists, the CIR produced papers that characterized the effect of big business on living conditions along lines much closer to the views of Ely than to those of Wright. The commission found that six major banking groups controlled three-quarters of the railroads and a quarter of manufacturing and that half "the wage-earners' families in the United States lacked sufficient income for adequate subsistence and health." These reports called for federal and state intervention on the side of unions and helped establish such government programs as labor exchanges, retraining schools, and public works. These programs were described as a prerequisite for ending labor unrest and for achieving distributive justice. They also outlined social insurance schemes covering sickness, unemployment, and old age to which employees, employers, and the government would jointly contribute (Furner 1990, 277).

2 :: The Early History of the NBER

The Prewar Origins of the NBER

As accounted in Herbert Heaton's *A Scholar in Action: Edwin F. Gay*, Jerome Greene, head of the Rockefeller Foundation, approached Edwin F. Gay and Frank Taussig of Harvard in 1914. The Rockefeller Foundation, which had long financed medical research, was interested in expanding to promote research in the social sciences. Greene proposed the establishment of a well-financed institute for economic research headed by a group of luminaries free to choose its own research agenda regardless of expense, with a well-paid director with as many associates as desired, a well-stocked library, and all other requisites (Heaton 1952, 91–92). Greene asked Gay and Taussig if such an organization would be likely to appeal to exceptionally talented scholars. Taussig was skeptical. He argued that the plan was too ambitious and that since enough good research was already being conducted in the universities the money would be better spent on existing institutions than on the competing institute that Greene proposed to establish.

Gay was more optimistic. He was an economic historian and the founding dean of Harvard's Graduate School of Business Administration, which had been established in 1908. He initiated the case method of study for the business school, brought Frederick Taylor, the founder of scientific management, to the faculty, and founded the Harvard Bureau of Business Research to help local businesses with their marketing. Gay believed that Taussig overestimated the quality and quantity of the research conducted at universities, most of which was individual and limited in scope. He therefore held that there was a place for

Greene's proposed institute and that it could attract top scholars provided it offered them satisfactory conditions. Encouraged by Gay's response, and with the approval of the trustees of the Rockefeller Foundation, Greene assembled a small group in New York in March 1914 to serve as an exploratory committee, with Gay as chairman.

Gay argued, in a memorandum prepared in June, that the proposed institute should not attempt any educational work directly but rather "strive to establish its reputation as a scientific, impartial and unprejudiced investigator" (Heaton 1968, 98–99) by undertaking studies that were beyond the scope of existing research universities and that would yield basic facts of interest to both economists and the public. He felt that these purposes would best be served by the collection of data on prices, wages, and rents and that Wesley Clair Mitchell should be placed in charge of this study. This proposal was submitted to the Rockefeller Foundation on August 4, 1914, the day World War I broke out in Europe. As might have been expected, the foundation recommended that, in light of the general preoccupation with the war, no further action be taken. Instead, it hired William Lyon MacKenzie King, an economist with a doctorate from Harvard University and former Canadian labor minister (and future prime minister), ostensibly to conduct research on American labor conditions but really to serve as an apologist for the Rockefeller family's labor policies. This approach proved a failure as both King and the Rockefellers were censured by the Congressional Committee on Industrial Relations. After the war, convinced by his advisers that funding the social sciences presented a simultaneous opportunity to benefit society and improve his public image, John D. Rockefeller Jr. arranged for the financing of some economic research projects but ensured that the family would be distanced from the conduct and results of that research. At that meeting, there was a prolonged discussion about what areas should be studied but "instant rejection of a suggestion by some outsiders that the institute embark on a campaign 'to teach the masses the fundamental ethical and economic principles underlying true prosperity'" (Heaton 1952, 92–93 [quote]; Smith 1994).

As explained in Fabricant (1984), the idea for an economic research institution came up again in 1916 when Malcolm Rorty, an employee of the American Telephone and Telegraph Company, approached Gay. Rorty wanted Gay to organize and direct a study of the volume and distribution of American income to be conducted by the Harvard Business School. Gay replied that such a study was too large for the school and that the best approach would be to found a body like the one Gay and Greene had independently proposed earlier. Rorty was added to this earlier group, and later Nahum Stone was brought on. Rorty and Stone made an unusual alliance. Rorty was an engineer and statistician with degrees in mechanical engineering and electrical engineering from Cornell University. Stone was an economist and statistician with a doctorate from Columbia University who early in his career had translated Karl Marx's *Contribution to the Critique of Political Economy* into English (see Marx 1904). The two had met in 1915 at a hearing in New York over a proposed state law establishing a minimum wage where Stone testified in favor of the proposed legislation while Rorty testified against it. In 1916, Stone reviewed Scott Nearing's *Income* (1915) for the *Intercollegiate Socialist*, a left-wing publication circulated among college students. Nearing was a socialist with a doctorate in economics from the Wharton School who had twice been fired from academic positions for his radical political views. In his book, Nearing divided all income into service and property income and concluded that national income was approximately evenly divided between the two types of income. In his review, Stone argued that Nearing had left out several components of service income from his calculations, including the earnings of clerks and other professionals, agricultural workers, and those employed in public service, transportation, trade, and domestic service and that in reality about 70 percent of all national income could be classified as service income.[1]

As Stone relayed the story at the twenty-fifth anniversary of the founding of the National Bureau of Economic Research, Rorty read his review and, expecting to "find a red hot diatribe on the unjust distribution of income under capitalism" (Stone quoted in Fabricant 1984, 4), was impressed by his objectivity and invited him to lunch.

---

1. Nearing's book was not well received by the profession. Besides Stone's review, see Adams (1916) and Young (1916).

The two agreed that more needed to be known about national income and its distribution and that an organization devoted to fact-finding on controversial economic questions of public interest would be of great benefit. They also agreed that the organization should be started by a group of well-known economists representative of every school of economic thought from extreme conservatism to extreme radicalism and to be led by a board of directors with representatives from all the country's organized interests. By June 1917, Rorty and Stone had formed the Committee on the Distribution of Income, which in addition to Gay included the economists Wesley Clair Mitchell of Columbia University, John R. Commons of the University of Wisconsin, Allyn Young of Cornell University, and T. S. Adams of Yale University as well as representatives from business and labor.

The group's objectives and plans were distributed in a memorandum stating that "the Committee [would] concern itself wholly with matters of fact, and [was] being organized for no other purpose and with no other obligation than to determine the facts and to publish its findings," and that it had "no conclusions or theories to advance and [assumed] no obligation to any subscriber other than to make and publish its determinations of fact." The entry of the United States into World War I diverted most of the committee's members to more urgent tasks. Stone headed the cost studies section in the office of the Quartermaster General of the Army, where he developed a new method of pricing government clothing contracts, eliminating the disadvantages of cost-plus agreements. Rorty served with the Ordnance Department and General Staff of the U.S. Army, with the task of purchasing ammunition and directing the shipment of arms. However, as will be seen, the war revealed the critical need for some type of institution to supply the organized statistical information about the economy needed for the country's urgent problems relating to war mobilization and reconstruction (Fabricant 1984).

The Role (and Limitations) of Economists in World War I

On June 3, 1916, the National Defense Act gave the president the authority to place orders for war matériel directly with suppliers, to commandeer plants for defense purposes if necessary, and to appoint an industrial mobilization board. Subsequently, the Council of National Defense, a spinoff of at least two organizations created by private funds, was created (Hughes and Cain 2002). Although its membership included government officials, most of its responsibilities were carried out by an advisory commission consisting of leaders from business and labor. The council's first director was Walter S. Gifford, chief statistician (and later the head) of the American Telephone and Telegraph Company. Other members included Bernard Baruch, a financier who would play a key role in organizing the American economy for both world wars, Samuel Gompers of the American Federation of Labor, and Julius Rosenwald, president of Sears Roebuck and Company. At the time the council was created, the U.S. Army did not even have plans for the equipment and organization of a large military force. To fill this void, the council insisted that the military make estimates of the requirements of a large army while the council itself estimated the country's resources and identified existing and potential scarcities.

This work was aided by the creation of the Commercial Economy Board in March 1917. Its chairman was Arch W. Shaw, a former publisher of business magazines (including one that would ultimately become *Business Week*), a founder of the Kellogg Company, and a lecturer at the Harvard Graduate School of Business Administration. Edwin Gay was also named to the board. The board's main responsibility was "to investigate and advise in regard to the effective and economical distribution of commodities among the civilian population" (Heaton 1968, 98–99), with the hope that it would find economies in civilian consumption to release labor for the military and reduce the civilian demand for materials needed by war industries. It did this mainly by attempting to find wasteful commercial practices and persuade manufacturers to abandon them. It had no enforcement powers, however, and hence had to appeal to patriotism.

After war was declared, the Council of National Defense attempted to bring the U.S. Army and the U.S. Navy together to coordinate purchases. In all previous wars, the two services had competed freely against each other in the market of goods. However, in the wake of industrialization, such a strategy would have resulted in bottlenecks that would have left tons of unfinished (and useless) military equipment clogging up production floors and warehouses. These attempts failed, however, and as a result the council created the War Industries Board in July 1917. It initially consisted of five civilians and one representative each of the army and the navy. However, it at first had no executive authority and failed to coordinate military purchases. It did not really become effective until after March 1918, when Bernard Baruch was made its head.

But, regardless of how efficient American production was or would become, the effort would have been of no use in World War I if supplies could not have been transported to Europe. When the United States entered the war, the assumption on both sides of the Atlantic had been that the chief American contribution would be money and munitions. But, after the defeat of the Italians at Caporetto in October 1917 and the withdrawal of the Russians from the war following the Bolshevik Revolution in November, which freed all German resources for the Western front, it became apparent that a much greater American commitment to the war would be necessary, which would require much greater shipping resources to get troops and matériel to the front.

It was the responsibility of the U.S. Shipping Board, established in September 1916, to find these resources. In August 1917, the board commandeered all hulls under construction in American yards and took control of all American ships over twenty-five hundred tons that were fit for use, creating the largest shipping concern in the world. However, ship operations were left in the hands of the owners, and the board made little attempt to direct these ships' comings and goings. As a result, "vessels were still in large measure free to go wherever there were good cargoes to be carried or picked up and fabulously profitable freights to be earned, especially on the routes to the markets that had been lost or deserted since 1914 by the British and Germans" (Heaton 1952, 105). To improve the board's effectiveness, it was imperative to improve the efficiency of ships already in service and to increase tonnage available for military use by restrictions on the importation of nonessential goods. In order to do this, three estimates were necessary: the probable tonnage requirements of the U.S. Army and its allies; the kind, quantity, and volume, in terms of ship space, of nonessential imports; and the cargoes, routes, capabilities, and performance of existing ships.

Unfortunately, none of these data were available. To rectify the situation, Edwin Gay was brought on in December 1917. He proceeded to interview members of the military, suppliers, and shippers and arrange for the collection of the necessary statistical data from the statistics departments of the Council of National Defense and the War Department and from the U.S. Mission to Paris. He estimated that an additional 3.6 million tons of deadweight shipping would be needed during the next six months in order to carry out the nation's military program and deliver essential supplies to the Allies (Cuff 1989, 597). One obstacle was that power was divided, with the Shipping Board allocating ships and the War Trade Board, which had initially been established in October 1917 to ensure that U.S. exports did not reach the enemy, approving imports. To solve this problem, the Ship Control Committee was created, bringing all ships controlled by the U.S. government (including the army) under centralized control. In February 1918, President Wilson declared that no goods could be imported without a government license. To put this program in place, the Division of Planning and Statistics was created within the Shipping Board, with Gay as its director, to gather information about ships and imports. These data were sent to the War Trade Board, of which Gay had been made a member. As one of two representatives of the Shipping Board who was on the War Trade Board, Gay could explain the findings and recommendations of his division to the latter organization. To aid him, he assembled a list of experts drawn from university professors and business leaders, including Wesley Clair Mitchell and Henry S. Dennison, a paper manufacturer, social reformer, and member of the scientific management movement who had helped Gay develop the curriculum at the Harvard Graduate School of Business Administration.

As director of the Division of Planning and Statistics, Gay had two responsibilities. The first was to prepare a list of restricted imports. To do this, Gay and his staff had to collect data on the nature and uses of imported commodities, alternative sources of supply, possible substitutes, stocks on hand, the shipping tonnage required for transportation to the United States, as well as the economic, financial, and political (both foreign and domestic) ramifications of restricting imports. Most of the data required for this analysis were severely lacking. For example, import statistics rarely gave country of origin or volume or weight of an imported commodity, making it difficult to calculate the ship tonnage space required for importation or the effect of the import ban on a friendly foreign power. Moreover, there were few data to show what happened to imports after they entered the country. In spite of this, the War Trade Board eventually put together a list of about two hundred imports to be restricted. By mid-1918, these restrictions released more than 1 million tons of shipping. This represented about 30 percent of the increase in shipping capacity for war purposes that Gay had originally called for or about 12 percent of the shipping under the Shipping Board's jurisdiction, which represented the lion's share of the shipping in the United States. Gay's second task was to ensure that the ships under the board's jurisdiction were used as efficiently as possible. This required the Division of Planning and Statistics to accumulate data on the complete inventory of every controlled ship and daily accounts of the movement of each ship to determine compliance with import restrictions, detect inefficiency in operations, and ensure maximum efficiency in the use of U.S. port facilities.

However, by mid-1918, a problem emerged. It was found that there was a large excess of actual shipping tonnage over that necessary for approved trade with South America and the Caribbean. When Gay reported this to P. A. S. Franklin, the chairman of the Ship Control Committee, Franklin informed Gay that this was no mistake and that Franklin intended to look after American interests in the Latin American market, even if this required flouting the import restrictions. To counter Gay, Franklin made a series of technical points in arguing that current shipping practices should remain unchanged, including that boats engaged in the Latin American trade were unfit for transatlantic shipping, that the surplus shipping to the area was only seasonal, and that triangular routing made his statisticians' analysis misleading.

The situation was exacerbated when Franklin made a public statement claiming that the British were still running ships exclusively for normal trade purposes in the western Atlantic while the United States had cut its trade to the bone, angering the British at a time when the United States was attempting to negotiate with them for the use of more of their ships (Heaton 1952, 119–23).

The situation came to a head on October 30 at the weekly meeting of the Tonnage Conference, which was attended by cabinet members, generals, admirals, and the chairmen of the relevant agencies. At this meeting, Franklin made his usual technical arguments to support the status quo. His colleagues from other government agencies, armed with data supplied by Gay, demolished his arguments and he was forced to concede defeat. As a result of the meeting, the Ship Control Committee was ordered to take all suitable vessels off nonessential trade routes at once, and the army insisted on reasserting control over the ships under its jurisdiction but agreed to let the Ship Control Committee operate them subject to advice from Gay and the War Trade Board rather than the Shipping Board. As a result of the meeting, several hundred thousand tons of shipping were taken out of civilian use and reallocated for military purposes. Although it is possible to exaggerate the importance of this episode (the October 30 meeting took place less than two weeks before the armistice was signed), it serves as one important example during World War I of an economist having an impact on policy, even over the objections of someone from an area with a more established hold on policy. It would foreshadow the much more important feasibility dispute of World War II (Heaton 1952, 119–23).

At around the time that the controversy with Franklin was developing, Gay was asked to create a division of planning and statistics for the War Industries Board. He found the organization's statistical apparatus to be in disarray. For example, there were no complete lists for either army contracts or steel suppliers. In addition to conducting several commodity studies, including an inventory of steel supplies, the division also established a price bureau under the direction of Wesley Clair Mitchell that produced price data for agencies controlling prices. It also helped conserve scarce resources for military consumption by persuading producers of consumer goods to reduce the number of styles of products, inducing manufacturers to use substitute materials for ones needed by war suppliers, and persuading the armed forces to standardize many of the products that they consumed. It also got the U.S. Army to centralize its purchases, which had previously been conducted by at least seven separate branches working independently of each other.[2]

Finally, in May 1918, President Wilson asked Bernard Baruch, head of the War Industries Board, if it would be possible to create "some kind of organization through which we could have a sort of picture . . . of all the present war activities of the Government and upon that base a periodical checking up of the actual operations and results?" (Wilson to Baruch cited in Duff 1989, 605). In response, Baruch asked the various government agencies producing statistics to provide data so that the War Industries Board could produce a general report. After facing resistance, particularly from the War Department, Gay, at the request of the assistant secretary, Franklin Roosevelt, established within the War Industries Board the Central Bureau of Planning and Statistics. He found most agencies' statements "almost entirely useless . . . They were more or less full of what the various departments were doing, all putting their best foot foremost" (Cuff 1989, 606). Moreover, many agencies continued to be reluctant to cooperate, particularly the army. However, the navy proved to be more cooperative, possibly as a result of the insistence of Roosevelt. To gain better data, Gay cultivated contacts in various government agencies and placed his own personnel with organizations that would accept them (Cuff 1989).

Another problem that Gay faced was the duplication of effort by the various federal agencies, with one agency collecting data that another already had, possibly in incompatible form. One consequence of this uncoordinated activity was that many businesses received multiple questionnaires from the federal government, frequently asking for the same information in such a form that the work had to be done

---

2. By the end of the war, Gay would also be named head of the War Trade Board's Bureau of Research and Statistics and chairman of the Statistical Committee in the Department of Labor. He was thus simultaneously the head of statistical divisions in five separate government organizations (Cuff 1989, 603; Heaton 1952, 125–26).

all over again. To solve these problems, Gay established the Statistical Clearing House to tell inquirers what data had already been collected and where they were available. He also attempted to centralize the submission of questionnaires to private businesses. But, since the Central Bureau did not produce statistics, its staff remained quite small, with approximately sixty employees. About half these were experts, including perhaps ten economists. The Central Bureau also produced a number of reports on topics such as the railroad and fuel situations and published a weekly newsletter, the *Weekly Statistical News*, listing statistical projects under way or recently completed. Although the war ended before the its policies could take full effect, the Central Bureau proved to be one of the most popular wartime agencies for business. Wesley Clair Mitchell's price bureau, for example, prepared a massive study of wholesale prices for about fifteen hundred commodities for the years 1917–18. Its research permitted both government policymakers and private businessmen to plan production and inventories. When the war ended, leading businessmen, administrators, and social scientists petitioned for the incorporation of the Central Bureau into the U.S. Department of Commerce. When President Wilson refused on the grounds that the government should not interfere in business, the NBER was established with private funds (Cuff 1989; Potter 1919; Smith 1994).

During World War I, the federal government practiced price control for the first time. In addition to the work of the Price Fixing Committee of the War Production Board, three other government organizations engaged in price control: the Food and Fuel Administrations and the Bureau of Transportation and Housing. The first three organizations were independent agencies responsible to the president, while the fourth was in the Labor Department. Although Bernard Baruch was made chairman of the Price Fixing Committee, prices were left outside his direct control, with the aim of separating price-fixing from other parts of the War Industries Board in order to cloak it with a quasi-judicial appearance. In part, this reflected President Wilson's aversion to concentrating economic power, and, in part, it was a response to critics who charged that the "dollar-a-year" men, War Industries Board volunteers from the private sector, remained loyal to the companies with which they had served before the war and that continued to pay their salaries. The board could not do without them, but they would not be allowed to use their power to gain excessively high prices for their firms. Although the Price Fixing Committee did little to stabilize the cost of living directly, it did reach a compromise with industry calling for the production of limited styles within certain price ranges (Rockoff 1984, 46–50).

The membership of the Price Fixing Committee reflected this intent; in addition to Baruch, the committee included representatives of labor, the U.S. Army and Navy, and the Federal Trade Commission. Other members included Robert S. Brookings, a prominent businessman, philanthropist, and founder of the Brookings Institution; Harry Garfield of the Fuel Administration; and Frank Taussig, one of America's leading economists, who had been consulted by Jerome Greene on the possible founding of an economic research institute. Taussig spent his entire academic career at Harvard University, from which he had received his doctorate in economics in 1883, and where he served as the editor of the *Quarterly Journal of Economics* for more than forty years. He first became known for *The Tariff History of the United States* (1882/2009), which went through seven subsequent editions and established him as the leading authority on U.S. tariffs. In 1911, he published *Principles of Economics*, which would become one of the leading textbooks in the United States and England. The fourth and final edition of this work appeared in 1939. Another important work was *International Trade*, published in 1927 and considered the first important book in that field. Despite his conservatism (he opposed a minimum wage for female workers and the federal income tax and was an advocate for hard money), Taussig encouraged dissenting viewpoints as an editor and teacher. He also served in several government posts on the local, state, and federal levels, the most important being as the first chairman of the U.S. Tariff Commission, a post he held from 1917 to 1920. In this capacity, his goal was to proceed cautiously from research to recommendations on the basis of facts that would supplant the political motives on which tariff legislation had been previously based (Keene 2000; Schumpeter, Cole, and Mason 1941). The position was particularly important because tariff revenues had been the dominant source of federal revenues until the passage of the Sixteenth Amendment to the U.S. Constitution in 1913, which allowed for the federal income tax.

In addition to the Price Fixing Committee, three other federal agencies dealt with price controls during World War I. The first was the Food Administration, which was dominated by Herbert Hoover as food administrator. His authority came from the Lever Act, which was as much concerned with excessive business profits as it was with price controls. It prohibited all "excessive" prices (namely, those that produced excessive profits) and, to enforce the prohibition, gave the food administrator the power to issue and revoke the licenses of dealers in commodities deemed necessary, to requisition commodities for the armed forces, and even to seize firms when necessary. For the most part, the Food Administration did not attempt to fix the prices of foodstuffs; rather, it limited the markups of middlemen and retailers to those prevailing in the prewar period in order to prevent war profiteering. Eventually, the it did impose price controls on a few commodities, the most important of which were sugar and wheat. A second agency applying price controls was the Fuel Administration, which had been set up in the summer of 1917 in response to a large spike in coal prices. It was headed by Harry Garfield, a lawyer and former president of Williams College. To control prices, the agency practiced bulk-line pricing, whereby the government set a price high enough to cover the costs and purchase the output of most of the nation's coal mines and then allocate it to military and civilian production and consumption. The exceptionally cold winter of 1917–18 saw the country's first energy crisis as a result of excessive demand for coal and the unusual demands on the railroad system imposed by the war effort. The Fuel Administration responded by closing all but a few coal-burning factories for several days, ordering nonessential industries such as breweries to cut back on their use of coal, and prohibiting the shipment of coal over long distances. The third federal organization that attempted to control prices during World War I was the Bureau of Transportation and Housing in the Department of Labor, but its enforcement powers were limited to appeals to patriotism, threats of punitive action by other government agencies, and the organization community committees to settle rental disputes (Rockoff 1984, 50–64).

The federal agencies set up in World War I to control prices accomplished their purpose. From May 1916 to August 1917, when controls were imposed, wholesale prices rose at an annual rate of 32.4 percent. After controls were imposed, the rise in wholesale prices fell to 7.1 percent per year. Although this was facilitated by a reduction in monetary expansion, monetary factors alone cannot account for the fall in inflation. Moreover, inflation was controlled "without the imposition of a large bureaucracy and without substantial damage to the productive side of the economy" (Rockoff 1984, 83).

World War I was a turning point in the use of economists in government. As the historian Ellis Hawley put it: "Economic inquiry for purposes of managing the economy as a whole had its real beginnings during World War I, at least insofar as it was done by credentialed professionals" (Hawley 1990, 288–89). Economists had, however, been used periodically by the federal government for congressionally authorized investigatory bodies, 25 specialists in economic and political science working for the federal government in 1896, a figure that rose to 848 during the Herbert Hoover administration (White 1933, 271–72).

Nevertheless, it is possible to overstate the influence of economists in this period. Altogether, about 120 members of the American Economic Association worked in Washington for the federal government during World War I, representing about 5 percent of the association's total membership (Fisher 1919).[3] This is not a large number given that some 5,000 government agencies were created during the war (Hughes and Cain 2007, 450). Moreover, with the possible exception of Edwin Gay, economists did not have much of an impact on policy. They were primarily used to assemble facts and statistics, which might or might not be used by policymakers. This fact was lamented by Jacob Hollander of Johns Hopkins University in his presidential address to the American Economic Association in 1921. Hol-

3. The membership total of 2,222 is taken from "Report of the Secretary" (see Fisher 1919, 357).

lander argued that, while physical scientists saw a rapid mobilization and the ready acceptance of their advice, the mobilization of economists was much slower and economic policy decisions were made by others. He complained: "Of the whole company of American economists, . . . not a single figure was in the first instance chosen . . . to exercise formative, determining influence in the economic conduct of the war" (Hollander 1922, 9). Even many of the top statisticians used in government came from business rather than academe. The limitation on the use of economists in World War I can be seen in the composition of the American delegation to the Paris Peace Conference. Although the Central Bureau was named as the official source of economic data for the American delegation, only two economists, Taussig and Allyn Young, were named to the delegation, which contained no representative of the Treasury Department, the War Industries Board, or any other agency that dealt with international economic questions.

The Founding of the NBER

In December 1918, the American Statistical Association (ASA) and the American Economic Association (AEA) held their joint annual meeting in Richmond, Virginia, in part to accommodate members who had been engaged in war work for the federal government (Alchon 1985, 38). The conference was, in particular, focused upon "C[redentialed] economic inquiry [that] a number of prominent government and business figures . . . believed could greatly enhance a society's capacity for planning" (Bernstein 2001, 40). The highlight of the meeting was presidential addresses by Wesley Clair Mitchell of the ASA and Irving Fisher of the AEA. Mitchell observed that World War I "led to the use of statistics, not only as a record of what had happened, but as a vital factor in planning what should be done." After the success of the application of statistics to problems of war, he suggested, statistics could be applied with equal success to problems of peace, and the application of statistics to the social sciences in the same way that it had already been applied in the physical sciences and industry could be used to achieve social harmony by promoting steady reform without class struggle. To do this, he called for the continuation of the Central Statistical Office or some similar organization "to consider the statistical needs of the government as a whole, . . . to lay systematic plans for meeting these needs," and to put relevant statistics "before the men whose decisions are important to the country, whether these men be administrators, legislators or voters" (Mitchell 1919, 234–35).

In his presidential address to the AEA, Irving Fisher called for the scientific study of the distribution of income and wealth and the causes of this distribution as a way of alleviating social conflict and argued that, provided that they maintained their independence and impartiality, economists would be in "the enviable position of being the logical arbiters in the class struggle now beginning—arbiters which both sides can trust." For this to happen, Fisher recommended the creation of two new agencies, "one designed to diffuse such economic knowledge as we possess, . . . the other designed to increase that knowledge." In order to accomplish this, he recommended:

> There should be created an endowment for economic research, in the management of which labor, capital and economists would . . . share, and which would be a sort of laboratory for the study of the great economic questions before us. Today the physical sciences have their great laboratories as a matter of course. But the economist is expected to secure his own facts and statistics and make his own calculations at his own expense. Expensive research, far beyond the reach of the professor's purse, is necessary if the economist is to be of any important public service in studying wealth distribution, the profit system, the problem of labor unrest, and the other many pressing practical problems. (Fisher 1919, 11, 19, 20)

As discussed, the groundwork for what would become the NBER had been laid before the U.S. entry into World War I, and the wartime experience revealed the lack of quantitative information necessary for the urgent needs of mobilization and reconstruction, thereby strengthening Malcolm Rorty's hand. In December 1919, the Commonwealth Fund, which had been chartered in 1918 by Stephen Harkness (whose father had been an early partner of John D. Rockefeller's) to "do something for the general welfare of mankind," had with some skepticism agreed to underwrite the new organization with a one-year grant of $20,000 (Alchon 1985, 56–57). The NBER was incorporated the following month with Edwin Gay as its first president. The charter stated that the organization was formed to "encourage, in the broadest and most liberal manner, investigation, research and discovery, and the application of knowledge to the well-being of mankind; and in particular to conduct . . . exact and impartial investigations in the field of economic, social and industrial science, and to this end to cooperate with governments, universities, learned societies and individuals" (Fabricant 1984, 7). The charter called for representation on the board of directors by appointment one member each of the AEA and the ASA as well as representatives of labor, employers, manufacturing, banking, farming, engineering, and the law. Initially, there were also plans for having representatives from the Federal Reserve Board and economics departments from various federal agencies, but these were dropped when the Commonwealth Fund objected that the appointments would be too political. In 1927, the economics departments of six universities—Harvard, Yale, Columbia, Chicago, Wisconsin, and Pennsylvania—would also have representatives on the board (Hawley 1990, 303). Initial directors at large included Edwin Gay, Wesley Clair Mitchell, T. S. Adams, John R. Commons, Allyn Young, and Nahum Stone. Directors by appointment included Arch Shaw and Malcolm Rorty; the latter succeeded Gay as president in early 1922.

Wesley Clair Mitchell was the NBER's first director of research, a position he held until 1945. After receiving his undergraduate degree from the University of Chicago, Mitchell stayed on at that institution to study philosophy and economics. The three teachers that he was most influenced by were the philosopher John Dewey and the economists Thorstein Veblen and J. Laurence Laughlin. Laughlin was the first chairman of the University of Chicago Economics Department and the founding editor of the *Journal of Political Economy*. He was a laissez-faire economist who opposed an inflationary expansion of the money supply and came to oppose the quantity theory of money. He interested Mitchell in monetary theory and suggested the federal government's issue of greenbacks, or paper currency, during the Civil War as a case study of the effect of paper money on an economic system. Mitchell found that the primary influence on prices was not the amount of greenbacks in circulation but the changing fortunes of the Union army. Moreover, by finding that during the Civil War real wages fell and nominal wages did not rise as fast as prices, Mitchell could show workers, to whom much of the inflationist propaganda was addressed, at least one case in which an inflationary monetary policy had been disastrous to their interests. More importantly, his thesis, published as *A History of the Greenbacks* (1903), was a pioneering work of statistics that showed the relation between money, prices, and wages (Smith 1994; Smith 2000).

Mitchell received his doctorate in economics from the University of Chicago in 1899 and left for the University of California, Berkeley, in 1903. While there, he became convinced that the future of economics lay in the collection of data and that the booms and busts of the capitalist economy were the nation's most pressing economic and social problem. He held that, if economists had sufficient information on business cycles, they could determine how the various aspects of the economy were interrelated and control these fluctuations. In *Business Cycles* (1913), he discussed the various theories about business cycles and provided detailed statistical records on business cycles between 1908 and 1911. This work demonstrated for the first time what statistical work could do. It was the first investigation of business cycles that permitted the investigation of the several factors at work simultaneously. Mitchell concluded that all the theories about contractions—excess savings, political uncertainty, tight money, overproduction, a decrease in construction, weather, and even sunspots—might be correct. Although he admitted that he could neither test these theories nor provide a new one that explained all the data he had gathered, he hoped that his work would provide the groundwork on which subsequent researchers could build (Smith 1994; Smith 2000).

Arthur Burns (1952, 23) called *Business Cycles* the most influential economic work between Marshall's *Principles of Economics* (1890) and Keynes's *General Theory* (1936), while John Maurice Clark (1931, 662) called it the "formative type" for the rise of quantitative economics. In

1913, Mitchell joined the faculty of Columbia University. In 1918, he helped found the New School for Social Research, where he taught for three years. He came to feel, however, that, because it did not grant degrees, the school was handicapped in attracting top students, so he returned to Columbia at the urging of his former colleagues (Dorfman 1959a, 360). He was the head of the AEA in 1925, and that organization awarded him the first Francis A. Walker Medal in 1947, given every five years (until 1977) to the individual who has contributed the most to the study of economics.

Under Gay and Mitchell's leadership, the NBER became immensely successful. While the Brookings Institution, which had been founded in 1916 as the first private research institute unaffiliated with a major university, achieved an enviable reputation as the result of the high quality of its research staff, its engagement with specific policy issues and its increasing identification with the Democratic Party gave it a reputation for partisanship (Bernstein 2001, 42). In contrast, the NBER insisted that its goal was to present economic facts in a scientific fashion, free from all bias and propaganda. Mitchell insisted that all reports be free of policy recommendations. The NBER as an institution had no opinion on social issues. To further ensure objectivity, each member of the board of directors had to approve a report before the bureau would accept and publish it. Moreover, any member of the board could append a qualifying or dissenting opinion to the report. These safeguards "effectively weeded out all opinions and recommendations; only a completely factual study could survive such scrutiny" (Smith 1994, 65). Moreover, all research was required to have public relevance and be practical in terms of understanding not just the economy as a whole but also the needs of the businessmen who funded the research.

National Income

The subject selected for the bureau's first study was that which had started the discussion between Rorty and Stone—the distribution of national income—but it was not limited to this. The size and industrial composition of national income were also examined, along with its growth and fluctuations beginning in 1909. To calculate real as well as nominal income, NBER staff went on to extend existing price indices as well as calculate new ones (Fabricant 1984, 11). This would be not only the most sophisticated assessment of national income yet produced but also the first comprehensive survey of the war's effect on the volume, contribution, and distribution of national income (Alchon 1985, 59). To ensure accuracy, two estimates were made, each based on separate data. The first approach, based on estimates of the commodities and services produced by all the extractive, transportation, manufacturing, financial, and government enterprises working in the United States, was conducted by Willford King, who had received his doctorate in economics from the University of Wisconsin in 1913 and worked as a statistician with the U.S. Public Health Service.

Using an eclectic mix of statistics, including "1901 worker survey data, 1902 Chicago Wages, 1914 Tax returns of top incomes, Wisconsin state income tax returns and other odds and ends," King had published his first estimate of national income in 1915 as *The Wealth and Income of the People of the United States*. The second approach, based on estimates of personal income together with the undistributed incomes of business and government, was led by Oswald Knauth. In June 1921, when the two independent estimates were compared for the period 1909–19, it was found that the largest discrepancy for any year was less than 7 percent and that the average discrepancy was only about 2 percent per year.

The study was published in 1921 and 1922 in two volumes, a small summary and a more detailed report of evidence and methods (NBER 1921b, 1922a).[4] The study concluded that per capita income was much larger in the United States than in any other country, that most of the increase in income occurring during World War I was due to an increase in prices, and that, while the distribution of income was highly inequitable, with the top 1 percent of income earners receiving 14 percent of all income and the top 5 percent of all income earners receiving 26 percent of all income, the war had acted to diminish income

---

4. A third volume, *Distribution of Income by States in 1919* (Knauth 1992), was also published.

inequality (NBER 1921b, 143–47). In the first annual report of the director of research to the Board of Directors, Mitchell concluded that national income was scarcely large enough to secure a decent standard of living for all American families and that the primary economic problem was to increase production and improve distribution of staple commodities (NBER 1921a, 10). Although the study did not receive widespread public attention, it was well received by the social science communities (Alchon 1985, 62–63). Writing in 1948, Arthur Burns concluded that the initial national income study "won public and professional support for the National Bureau in its early years of struggle" (quoted in Fabricant 1984, 11) and, as Fabricant put it, "more than anything else, helped to establish the reputation of the Bureau for thoroughness of work" (1984, 11).

The President's Conference on Unemployment

In 1920 and 1921, the United States suffered its worst contraction since the 1890s. Following a vigorous postwar boom, the Federal Reserve, facing a decline in its gold reserves, sharply raised the discount rate. At the same time, government spending declined by more than 70 percent in nominal terms from 1919 to 1921, and agricultural prices fell sharply as European production recovered from the war. As a result, nominal net national product fell by 18 percent from 1920 to 1921 (the drop in real terms was 4 percent), while unemployment rose to 11.7 percent in 1921 (its highest rate since 1898) (Hughes and Cain 2007, 444–54; Rockoff and Walton 2005, 427–28; U.S. Bureau of the Census 1975, 135).

In response to the contraction of 1920–21, Herbert Hoover, the new secretary of commerce under President Warren Harding, convened the President's Conference on Unemployment. Hoover, who served as secretary of commerce from 1921 to 1928 and who, according to a colleague, considered himself "Undersecretary of all other departments" (Barber 1985, 5), may have been one of the most powerful cabinet members of all time. He dominated the conference by setting the agenda and by carefully selecting the participants (Alchon 1985, 76). He also asked the NBER to prepare the conference's report on unemployment and business cycles within six months. Gay replied that since the topic dealt with issues that the bureau had already planned to undertake—as mentioned, Mitchell was one of the country's foremost authorities on business cycles—the NBER would undertake the work provided that the report would be submitted to the NBER's Board of Directors for approval before being sent to the conference, that the NBER would be free to publish its findings separately if it so desired, that the report would be confined to ascertaining facts, and that the money could be found to meet the bureau's expenses. Hoover agreed to the conditions and arranged for the Carnegie Corporation to provide a $50,000 grant to finance the study (NBER 1922b, 6–7). The study was prepared by the NBER's own staff and outside experts from universities, private organizations and charities, and U.S. government agencies.

The study was released as *Business Cycles and Unemployment* (Committee on Business Cycles and Unemployment 1923). Hoover wrote the introduction. It emphasized the importance of the dissemination of statistical information if business cycles were ever to be brought under control. It also stressed the need to use public and private construction funds countercyclically to moderate the effect of booms and busts while noting the critical role that the Federal Reserve could play in moderating the business cycle. But what the report emphasized most was the role of the individual businessman in moderating the business cycle by avoiding excessive expansion during booms and excessive contraction (including cutting nominal wages) during busts. Public reaction to the study was mixed: business and social science reviewers expressed approval, while the reform community was disappointed with the report's failure to endorse compulsory unemployment insurance (Alchon 1985, 107–8), which Hoover strongly opposed. Throughout the 1920s and 1930s, he remained opposed to both laissez-faire capitalism and bureaucratic coercion, preferring voluntary cooperation among private organizations and labor as a way to lessen the swings of the business cycle and to avoid class conflict.

In addition to the final report, the NBER also published a second book resulting from its work for the President's Conference on Unemployment. In planning its survey of cyclic unemployment, the bureau found that there was no consensus on what the number of unemployed actually was in 1921, with estimates ranging from 2.1 to 5 million. To rectify this situation, Willford King was put in charge of a study estimating the number of people employed in every quarter from 1920 to March 1922. With the cooperation of three federal agencies (the Department of Agriculture, the Bureau of the Census, and the Bureau of Railway Economics) and of many private organizations and individuals, King obtained the most accurate figures to date on employment, finding that the total number of employees on all payrolls had shrunk by about one-seventh between the third quarter of 1920 and the third quarter of 1921 and that total employment in hours fell by about one-sixth (King 1923).

Government Agencies Performing Economic Analysis in the 1920s

The major federal agencies performing economic analysis during the 1920s were the Bureau of Agricultural Economics (located in the Department of Agriculture) and the Bureau of the Census and the Bureau of Foreign and Domestic Commerce (both located in the Department of Commerce), the Bureau of Labor Statistics (located in the Department of Labor), and the Federal Reserve Board (an independent agency). The most important functions of the federal government requiring economic analysis were managing the nation's money and banking system through the Federal Reserve and providing aid to farmers as they struggled through the 1920s (Duncan and Shelton 1978, 13).

When Henry C. Wallace (a former editor of a leading agricultural magazine and the father of Henry A. Wallace, who would serve as vice president in the third Franklin Roosevelt administration) became secretary of agriculture in 1921, he was "convinced of the importance for agriculture of economic analysis by statistical methods." To that end, he combined three existing bureaus within the Department of Agriculture into the Bureau of Agricultural Economics (BAE). This agency soon became recognized for the quality of its staff, which developed and applied correlation and regression methods earlier than any other federal agency. In most other agencies, analysis was limited to the compilation of statistics, with masses of clerks transcribing and totaling raw data. There was no scientific sampling, no federal national income and product accounts (except for a onetime study in 1926 by the Federal Trade Commission), and no interagency coordination. Although punch-card machines had been invented, their use in the federal government was extremely limited (Duncan and Shelton 1978, 10 [quotation], 14).

By 1924, the BAE established a public research institute, complete with a research director, a graduate school, and research projects. However, the BAE quarreled with two of the most important leaders in the collection of statistics during the 1920s, the NBER and Herbert Hoover. Many of the BAE studies were linked to an emerging theory of agricultural economics that rejected laissez-faire remedies for agricultural distress, seeking instead to use the government to restrict agricultural output. Hoover and, to a lesser extent, the NBER saw the BAE as a political agency (rather than a scientific one) whose claims of disinterestedness and economic analysis were tainted by its political views. Hoover ultimately succeeded in having the head of the BAE ousted, and the organization became more circumspect in its policy prescriptions (Hawley 1990, 296, 310–12).

When Herbert Hoover became secretary of commerce, he directed the Bureau of the Census to collect the available data on the production, stocks, sales, and prices of various commodities and to make the data available for use by business by publishing them in a new monthly publication, the *Survey of Current Business*. Originally, the *Survey of Current Business* included little original material; it assembled various current economic statistics from government sources, commercial journals, and trade associations and put them into more useful form. Over the course of the 1920s, the Bureau of the Census began compiling its own statistics for many industries. The Bureau of Foreign and Domestic Commerce (BFDC), which had been created within the Department of Commerce in 1913, was the other major bureau within the department conducting economic analysis during Hoover's tenure as secretary. The BFDC's most important work during the decade started in 1923, when it began issuing estimates of the balance of payments, which was one of the first examples of the preparation and publication by the federal government of economic estimates rather than mere compilations (Duncan and Shelton 1978, 11).

As mentioned previously, the data on unemployment in the early 1920s were particularly bad. At the President's Conference on Unemployment, when the question of the number of unemployed people came up, the matter was actually put to a vote among the conference participants. One reason for the lack of data on labor was that the subject was largely seen as a state and local rather than a federal matter. The federal agency primarily responsible for the collection of such data was the Bureau of Labor Statistics, but before the Great Depression it was small and conducted research only on an ad hoc basis, with monthly published data limited to employment and payrolls in manufacturing along with some data on prices (Duncan and Shelton 1978, 18–19). The final federal agency responsible for economic analysis during the 1920s, the Federal Reserve Board, collected weekly data on the money supply and debits, or claims against the deposits of, member banks. However, there were few data on nonfarm real estate and mortgages, or on who borrowers were, or what the loans were used for.

Role of Private Foundations

Private foundations played a crucial role in the founding of the NBER. Among the philanthropic organizations funding the social sciences in the period between World War I and the Great Depression were the Carnegie Corporation, the Russell Sage Foundation, and the Commonwealth Fund. However, the most important was the Laura Spelman Rockefeller Memorial Fund, which funded the NBER along with the Social Science Research Council (SSRC) and the Brookings Institution, and which was responsible for much of the fortyfold increase in philanthropic support for the social sciences that occurred during this period (Alchon 1985, 117). From 1922 until 1929, the head of the Spelman Fund was Beardsley Ruml, a University of Chicago Ph.D. in psychology and education who had helped develop the U.S. Army's aptitude tests during World War I and who would later serve as the dean of the University of Chicago's Division of Social Sciences. In an important memorandum written shortly after becoming head of the Spelman Fund, he suggested guidelines for the funding of research in the social sciences, holding that the fund should support only empirical research that had practical applications. Under his guidance, the fund distributed more than $58 million for research in the social sciences during the 1920s (Smith 2000, 26–27). To avoid controversies such as the MacKenzie King affair discussed previously, Ruml "refused to fund organizations concerned with legislation, to become involved in any social or economic reform, to try to influence findings or even deal directly with researchers, or to fund non-empirical studies" (Smith 2000, 26).

Along with other philanthropic organizations, the Spelman Fund provided the initial funding for the SSRC. The SSRC was founded in 1923, with representatives from the American Political Science Association, the AEA, the ASA, and the American Sociological Society to encourage coordination and collaboration among the social sciences. Its first projects were efforts to improve government statistics, to support cooperative research on the subjects of immigration, agriculture, and crime, and to conduct a joint analysis of research methods and their complementarity throughout the social sciences. Its goal "was a social science capable of the kind of analysis 'so common in the natural sciences where the same subject is attacked by a variety of research workers simultaneously from different angles, where the same question is subjected to repeated investigations, and where comparative studies are the order of the day'" (Alchon 1985, 114–16).

The physical manifestation of the ideas of the Spelman Fund and the SSRC was the construction of the Social Science Research Building at the University of Chicago, completed in 1929. Paid for by the Spelman Fund, it represented Ruml's vision of the ideal physical setting for the social sciences. Floor space was flexible to allow for the development of cooperative, interdisciplinary research. There were only a few lecture rooms and no space at all for books, and most of the rooms were filled with gadgets to measure and enumerate data (Smith 2000, 28). Under the bow window of the Fifty-Ninth Street side of the building were chiseled the words of Lord Kelvin: "When you can measure what you are speaking about, and express it in numbers, you know something about it; but when you cannot measure it, when you cannot express it in numbers, your knowledge is of a meager and unsatisfactory kind."

Committee on Recent Economic Changes

The United States had enjoyed fairly steady economic growth and rising living standards since 1921, while Europe was undergoing labor unrest, debt and exchange problems, and recurrent economic contractions. Because of this success, Herbert Hoover argued that it was time to reconvene another unemployment conference to study the progress that had been made since the depression of 1920–21. He was also concerned that the general prosperity was hiding dangerous developments, such as weakness in agriculture, textiles, and coal mining. As a result, the Committee on Recent Economic Changes was convened in late 1927. Its secretary saw the committee as a kind of private national planning board, composed of senior "public men" advised by a permanent staff of skilled economists, engineers, and other professionals, whose purpose would be "to submit to the public not simply basic facts, but plans of action" (Alchon 1985, 132). Once again, the NBER was called on to write the committee's report, with expenses to be met by grants of $75,000 each from the Carnegie Corporation and the Spelman Fund. However, unlike the previous President's Conference on Unemployment, which had been at least nominally directed privately, the Committee on Recent Economic Changes was to be organized by the federal government, with Hoover as the chairman.

The committee first met in February 1928, and its report was published a little over a year later (see Committee on Recent Economic Changes 1929). In addition to the NBER, about thirty scientific, labor, and professional organizations and over thirty colleges and universities and nine government agencies provided, with the chapters based on this information written by the NBER's staff along with eleven outside experts chosen to study particular topics (Alchon 1985, 146). The report attributed most of the growth since 1921 to improvements in the training and practice of managers and an increase in consumption resulting from higher incomes, consumer credit, and mass advertising, which had been sufficient to absorb the increase in production that had brought about the growth of the 1920s. Although it noted that employment in manufacturing had declined owing to increases in productivity, that industry concentration had increased, and that certain industries, particularly agriculture, remained distressed, it concluded that, as long as demand remained strong, continued prosperity was likely (Barber 1985, 66–68; Alchon 1985, 149). Although the report was well received, it contained no hint of the coming cataclysm and would later be faulted as hurried and ill considered, subject to too much pressure from an arbitrary deadline imposed by Hoover (Alchon 1985, 148–50).

3 :: The Emergence of National Income Accounting as a Tool of Economic Policy

Herbert Hoover was sworn in as president at the end of a decade of generally vigorous economic growth, marred by the deep but short recession of 1920–21. By March 1929, the economy was near the top of a vigorous boom. In his inaugural address, Hoover was lyrical in his vision of American prosperity: "Ours is a land rich in resources; stimulating in its glorious beauty; filled with millions of happy homes; blessed with comforts and opportunity. In no nation are the institutions of progress more advanced. In no nation are the fruits of accomplishment more secure. In no nation is the government more worthy of respect. No country is more loved by its people. I have an abiding faith in their capacity, integrity, and high purpose. I have no fears for the future of our country. It is bright with hope" ("Inaugural Address" 1929). However, that bright hope received a terrible jolt just seven months later with the stock market crash of October. In 1930, the unemployment rate jumped to nearly 9 percent, triple the rate of the previous year. During 1932, Hoover's last full year in office, nearly a quarter of the labor force was out of work (Smiley 1983).

Hoover did not fiddle while Rome burned. He had been an activist secretary of commerce for eight years, and he moved far more forcefully to influence the course of the economy than any previous president.

Because the agricultural sector was depressed when he assumed office, Hoover supported the establishment of the Federal Farm Board with authority to lend money to farmers and promote farm cooperatives. Concern with the speculative stock market boom of 1927–28, fueled by the low interest rates of the New York Federal Reserve Bank, led him to pressure the bank to desist in lowering rates and also to seek new regulations to limit margin buying and insider trading. Because of the stock market crashes of October 24 and November 29, Hoover feared that a major cyclic downturn was impending, and he sought to counter it with a reduction in taxes and expanded public works. He also held a series of conferences, organized with the help of the NBER, that involved representatives of business, labor, and government to address the impending recession ("American President: Herbert Hoover," n.d.).

Because he expected the economic downturn of 1930–31 to be similar to that of 1920–21 (sharp but brief), Hoover initially opposed major federal intervention. However, the large rise in bank failures and a huge jump in unemployment led him to support legislation establishing a vigorous public works program and temporary emergency relief. He also supported prolabor legislation curtailing injunctions against strikes and confirming the right of workers to organize in unions ("American President: Herbert Hoover," n.d.).

In addition to legislation and executive orders, Hoover engaged in extensive jawboning, organizing conferences of business, labor, and academics aimed at persuading large corporations not to cut wages and unions not to strike. These efforts, in which the NBER played a major role, were surprisingly effective.

Nevertheless, the rate of bank failures rose to unprecedented levels, and, by 1932, unemployment was eight times the level of 1929 (one of every four industrial workers was unemployed). Hoover sought to stem the decline in the economy by deficit spending, doubling the national debt, which reached 40 percent of GNP in 1932 (Gay and Mitchell 1929, 1933; NBER 1931, 1932; "United States Unemployment Rate," n.d.).

The New Deal

During the election of 1932, Roosevelt railed against the shocking escalation of federal government spending by Hoover and his expansion of the federal bureaucracy. Roosevelt's running mate, John Nance Garner (the speaker of the U.S. House of Representatives), accused Hoover of "leading the country down the path of socialism" (Otto, Gorey, and Galvin 1982, 26). The recurrent themes of Roosevelt's campaign were a return to laissez-faire and fiscal solvency at all levels of government.

After his inauguration, however, Roosevelt unleashed a fury of measures aimed at turning the economy around through "relief, recovery, and reform." Much of this program was formulated before he took office by his "brain trust," academic advisers trained in economics and corporate law and connected to Columbia University.[1]

During his first hundred days in office, Roosevelt concentrated on overcoming the banking panic. The day after his inauguration, Congress passed legislation for a "bank holiday," which stopped the run on the banks, and then established the Federal Deposit Insurance Corporation, which provided federal insurance of deposits if banks failed. He also extended Hoover's relief programs under the supervision of a new agency, the Federal Emergency Relief Organization.

To remove single, young, unemployed men from the labor market, he established the Civilian Conservation Corps to work on construction projects in rural areas. Congress also broadened the antimonopoly powers of the Federal Trade Commission, and the powers of Hoover's Reconstruction Finance Commission were extended to permit government financing of industry and railroads. The Agricultural Adjustment Administration was established to raise farm prices by paying farmers to take land out of production and reduce the size of herds.

The National Industrial Recovery Act (NIRA), which became law on June 16, 1933, was the main instrument used by Roosevelt in his attempt to reorganize the economy. The act permitted the president to establish the Public Works Administration, which initiated construction projects that included the Boulder Dam (now Hoover Dam) in

---

1. Roosevelt's original brain trust included Adolf Berle (corporate law), Raymond Moley (political science), Rexford Tugwell (economics), and James Warburg (banking). Berle, Moley, and Tugwell all taught at Columbia University.

Colorado and the New York Triborough Bridge (now the Robert F. Kennedy Bridge).

The main feature of NIRA was its Title I, which permitted the president to cartelize industry and require farmers to take land out of production. To implement NIRA, leaders of each industry were asked to design codes to control economic activity by maintaining prices and wages, production, and employment. The aim of the program was to raise prices by reducing production, and, initially, it had the desired effect. But, after the fall of 1933, implementation of the program became sporadic as firms stopped cooperating. The increase in economic activity stalled between the fall of 1933 and 1935, when the Supreme Court declared NIRA unconstitutional (Smiley, n.d.; Romer 1993, 1999).

The 1934 congressional elections gave Roosevelt large majorities in both houses of Congress. Among the legislation that emerged was the bill creating the Works Progress Administration (WPA), which employed 2 million workers, including many writers, artists, and actors. The WPA put actors to work in roving theaters that performed in local neighborhoods, and the artists painted murals on the walls of public buildings. More important in its impact on labor was the National Labor Relations Act of 1935, which gave a powerful impetus to workers to engage in collective bargaining through trade unions. That act prohibited employers from blocking the activities of unions and required employers to bargain with representatives of unions. It established the National Labor Relations Board to enforce the act.

It has become something of a legend that the high level of government spending under Roosevelt pulled the economy forward. Indeed, between 1932 and 1936, real GNP increased at over 7.5 percent per year. It is also true that deficit spending at the federal level remained high. The decline in unemployment from 25 percent of the labor force in 1933 to about 14 percent in 1937 has also been attributed to fiscal policy. Somewhat puzzling, then, is the 1938 rise to 19 percent of unemployment, which lingered above 14 percent through the end of 1940, when Roosevelt promised to make America "the Arsenal of Democracy."

Overall, fiscal policy had little effect on the recovery from the Depression. During most years of Roosevelt's first two terms, there were substantial increases in local, state, and federal taxes. Although government spending increased between 1933 and 1939, in all these years except 1936 taxes exceeded government expenditures. While the federal government ran deficits, state and local governments had offsetting surpluses. As E. Cary Brown of the Massachusetts Institute of Technology (a specialist in public finance) put it, fiscal policy was unsuccessful in promoting recovery from the Depression, "not because it did not work, but because it was not tried" (Brown 1956, 863, 866).

The growth of the U.S. military was a major factor inhibiting unemployment. In 1933, less than a quarter of a million men were in the armed forces. By 1940, the figure had doubled, and, by 1941, the last peacetime year (Congress did not declare war until December 8), the armed forces had quadrupled. The armed forces and the armament industries soaked up much of the pool of unemployed workers (U.S. Bureau of the Census 1975, chap. D, esp. ser. D1–10).

The Federal Government Assumes Responsibility for the National Income Accounts

In June 1932, reeling from the prolonged recession, the U.S. Senate passed a resolution calling on the Department of Commerce to provide estimates of U.S. national income for the years 1929–31. Since there was no one in the Department of Commerce who was familiar with the construction of national income accounts, the department called on the NBER for help. By 1930, Simon Kuznets, who had become the principal investigator in this area at NBER, was "loaned" to the Department of Commerce to accomplish this task.

In January 1933, Kuznets established a working group at the Department of Commerce that included Robert R. Nathan, one of his former graduate students at the University of Pennsylvania. Kuznets's work on this project was informed by his command of welfare theory, which provided the basis for his estimating procedures. He also carefully checked and rechecked the work of his assistants in several ways. Kuznets, extremely well organized, not only completed the report within a year but also provided estimates for 1932, one year more than requested by the Senate. The printed report had a main section of 157 pages and over 100 pages of additional material. "Both in accuracy and in wealth of detail, this report was far ahead of anything yet produced on national income," wrote two historians of government statistics (Duncan and Shelton 1978).

Kuznets's report was well received by a number of government agencies, which began to make use of the national income concept. It was also widely used by business organizations for market analysis and in the research of academic economists. Press coverage of the report was substantial, and sales of the report to the public exceeded those of the *Statistical Abstract* (Duncan and Shelton 1978).

In December 1934, Nathan was asked to return to the Commerce Department, where he became chief of a permanent national income section (later a separate division). He thoroughly reviewed and updated the earlier work in addition to producing new annual estimates of national income and related statistics, including unemployment. In June 1940, he was asked to shift to the newly established National Defense Advisory Commission, which advised Roosevelt on the U.S. military buildup (Edelstein 2001; Robert Nathan, in discussion with the Fogels, 1990; Carson 1990).

Making America the Arsenal of Democracy

On December 29, 1940, President Roosevelt delivered a speech aimed at building popular support for the British struggle against the Nazis. By that date, most of Europe, including France, was under Nazi control. British cities suffered heavy bombing attacks, and, after capturing the British Channel Islands, Hitler was poised to invade the British mainland.

Roosevelt warned: "If Britain goes down, the Axis powers [Germany, Italy, and Japan] will control the continents of Europe, Asia, Africa, Austral-Asia, and the high seas. And they will be in a position to bring enormous military and naval resources against this hemisphere." We would, he continued, "be living at the point of a gun," and we could survive only by converting ourselves "permanently into a militaristic power on the basis of war economy." The oceans could no longer protect us from overseas aggression because advances in technology made it possible for bombers to fly from Europe and back without refueling. Calling on workers and managers of plants to cooperate in producing the needed armaments, Roosevelt promised a proper division between aiding Britain and U.S. national defense. Making ourselves "the great arsenal of democracy," he said, was both patriotic and correct policy (Roosevelt 1940).

Roosevelt's speech had a powerful effect on mobilizing the country for war. It precipitated a new globalism in place of the isolationist doctrine that prevailed after World War I. It also made it possible to expand greatly the number of men under arms, from 458,000 in 1940 to 1,801,000 a year later (U.S. Bureau of the Census 1975, chap. Y, ser. Y 904–16).[2]

Roosevelt's call to the nation was not the beginning of the U.S. mobilization for war. Although he ran his reelection campaign of 1940 on the promise not to involve the United States in another European war, the president began the mobilization for war in May 1940, with the establishment of the National Defense Advisory Commission (NDAC), whose mission was to mobilize industry and the nation for war. In June, Robert Nathan was asked to become the associate director of the NDAC, where he worked closely with the director, Stacy May, an economist, on the task of determining what the military requirements would be under alternative assumptions about the scope of U.S. engagement in the war. However, the planners at the army and navy were not interested in cooperating (Nathan 1994).

Nathan, therefore, spent the balance of 1940 working on what GNP would be at full employment, a project with which some of the military planners were cooperative. The analysis took account of the fact that one-seventh of the labor force was still unemployed and of the continuing underutilization of plant capacity. Nathan and his team estimated that, at full employment, 45 percent of GNP would be absorbed by the military, with the rest available for essential civilian activities. Within that context, they then estimated at what level of GNP critical

2. The rapid increase in the armed forces was facilitated by the Selective Service and Training Act, which passed Congress in September 1940.

shortages would arise. They focused on steel (needed for tanks, ships, and guns), aluminum (needed for airplanes), and copper (needed for munitions). On the basis of this analysis, plans were developed for the stockpiling of critical materials, the building of new plants and equipment, and the allocation of products for civilians (Robert Nathan, in discussion with the Fogels, 1990; Nathan 1994).

The steel industry leaders initially rejected the call for expansion of their plants because only a few years earlier they were operating at just 20 percent of capacity and were still well below capacity in 1940. Moreover, they expected that, after the war, the economy would return to the conditions of the Great Depression and they would be stuck with even greater overcapacity than previously. The government responded by offering attractive incentives, and, by the time Pearl Harbor was attacked, steel capacity was up by nearly 15 percent (Nathan 1994).

In the case of aluminum, the sole producer, the Aluminum Company of America (also known as ALCOA) did greatly expand its capacity. The government also aided in the establishment of two new aluminum companies, the Reynolds Company and Kaiser Aluminum. Jointly, these companies provided the output to create the large stockpiles required to accelerate military production at remarkable rates after the bombing of Pearl Harbor.

In June 1941, Roosevelt called on the army, the navy, and the Maritime Commission to estimate resource needs in the event of a war. The resulting estimates were combined into a plan that came to be called the "Victory Program" and were sent to the president in the early fall. After the attack on Pearl Harbor, Roosevelt used the Victory Program to formulate his objectives for war production in 1942 and 1943. In his State of the Union Address to Congress on January 6, 1942, he announced his "must list" of production targets for 1942: 60,000 planes, 45,000 tanks, and 6 million tons of shipping. For 1943, the goals were 125,000 planes, 75,000 tanks, and 10 million tons of shipping.

The question then became, Were these production goals feasible? If the goals were too high, they would result in many tanks without treads and many planes without propellers because not all components could be increased at the same rate. In deciding this issue, there was a fundamental disagreement between civilian economists and senior military officials. The economists argued that the military's goals were unrealistic and would result in resources being squandered on parts that could not be used. The issue was ultimately decided by the Roosevelt administration, which sided with the economists (Brigante 1950; Edelstein 2001; Smith 1959).

That question was put to the Planning Committee of the War Production Board, of which Nathan was chairman and Kuznets chief economist. Kuznets prepared a highly classified memorandum using national income techniques to show that much more could be produced with ambitious but attainable goals than with unattainable goals. Eventually, the planners within each of the armed services were convinced to accept the lower production goals adopted by the War Production Board (Nathan 1994; Edelstein 2001).

World War II was by far the most extensive dedication of economic resources to war in American history. Out of a labor force of 60 million, more than a third were either in the armed forces or engaged in war production. World War II was also an exceedingly bloody war. All told, there were about 60 million deaths, one-third military and two-thirds civilian, with about 85 percent on the Allied side and 15 percent on the Axis side (Nathan 1994).

The Economist's War

Although the use of national income accounting to allocate resources between military and civilian needs was the most important contribution of economists to victory in World War II, it was not their only one. Economists played a major role in several wartime agencies, including the Office of Price Administration (OPA), the Office of Strategic Services (OSS), and the Statistical Research Group (SRG).

The OPA was established by executive order in April 1941 and then by congressional act in January 1942. Its mission was to control ceilings on all prices other than agricultural commodities and to otherwise ration scarce supplies of such important consumer products as tires, shoes, nylon, sugar, gasoline, coffee, and meats. Much of this rationing was done by the issuance of food stamps to consumers, who had to present the coupons along with money to purchase rationed items such as meat.

The first head of the OPA was Leon Henderson, an adviser to Roosevelt on economic issues. John Kenneth Galbraith was second in command from 1942 to 1943, when he was forced out by conservatives in Congress who disliked the style and content of his policies (John Kenneth Galbraith, in discussion with the Fogels, 1990).

The OSS was the predecessor to the current CIA. Its aim was to collect and analyze all information bearing on national security. The agency was divided into three divisions responsible for specific geographic regions: Europe-Africa, the Soviet Union, and the Far East. Each regional division had an economics subdivision. In addition, the deputy director of the OSS, Edward Mason of Harvard University, was an economist. The table of organization included a unit that created national income estimates for the German economy as a tool to evaluate the Nazis' productive and military capacity. The OSS economists' estimates proved to be highly accurate (Guglielmo 2008).

The SRG at Columbia University was focused on the practical application of statistics to military problems. Among the eighteen professionals were two economists who would later become Nobel Laureates in economics, Milton Friedman and George Stigler, and two statisticians, W. Allen Wallis and Abraham Wald. Wallis's contributions included the invention of several new statistical techniques as well as the elevation of statistical analysis in graduate business programs. He was also the chairman of the committee that recommended that the recruitment to the armed forces should be based on well-paid volunteers rather than low-paid draftees. Wald is best known for his book *Sequential Analysis*, which provides answers to the question, How many successive observations of a new weapon are needed to make a sound decision about the effectiveness of its design? (Wald 1947; see also Guglielmo 2008; Warsh 2003).

Milton Friedman looked at the problem of the optimal number and size of pellets in an aircraft shell, finding that a large number of small pellets was optimal. He also studied proximity fuses, which are tiny radars built into antiaircraft shells that cause the shell to explode within a predetermined distance of an aircraft. The problem was to avoid being too close to the plane, because then the shell might miss, or too far, because then the pellets of the shell would be going too slowly to do much damage. As a result of this work, the effectiveness of shells was more than doubled (Guglielmo 2008).

Restoring Europe

Europe was devastated immediately after the close of World War II. Blanket bombings destroyed major cities, with factories especially hard-hit. Also hit-hard were railways, bridges, and docks, and much merchant shipping had also been destroyed. Labor was malnourished and in disarray. Food was particularly short during the severe winter of 1946–47, and millions of refugees were kept alive with food supplied by the United Nations.

Impeded by labor strikes, the recovery was slow. In 1947, European economies were well below prewar levels and stagnating. Agricultural production and industrial production were more than 10 percent below their 1938 levels, and exports were off by over 40 percent. Housing shortages were severe, partly because of the large amount of housing that had been destroyed, and partly because of the stream of refugees flowing into Western Europe from Eastern Europe.

By the middle of 1947, the Truman administration realized that it could not let the German economy continue to deteriorate under the regime of deliberate economic neglect that it had been pursuing. It concluded that economic recovery in Europe required the contribution of a healthy German economy. In July 1947, when Gen. George C. Marshall became secretary of state, the decree that aimed at punishing Germany was scrapped. The new decree stated that a prosperous Europe required a productive and stable Germany. Some of the restrictions placed on German heavy industry were lifted. By the end of 1947, the United States declared that a general revival of German industry was of primary importance to U.S. national security.

On June 5, 1947, in a commencement address at Harvard University, Marshall proposed that American financial aid should be offered to assist in the European recovery. The offer was rejected by the Soviet Union and the Eastern Bloc countries but cautiously welcomed by the West European nations. In the ensuing negotiation, the Europeans were encouraged to develop their own plan for how U.S. aid would be used. Congress allocated $12.4 billion to be spent over four years, beginning in 1948.

Over the four years of the Marshall Plan, the European economy grew vigorously. These years witnessed the fastest rate of increase in European history, with industrial production rising by 35 percent. There has been considerable debate over whether the Marshall Plan was necessary for this swift recovery. In any case, the rapid growth continued for another two decades.

Economic historians now refer to the years between 1950 and 1973 as an economic golden age for Western Europe. Per capita income grew at a rate of 3.4 percent, well above the rate for any previous or subsequent period of similar length for the region. During this period, Western Europe, which had already recovered its prewar level by 1950, more than doubled its per capita income (Maddison 2006).

The American Century

In February 1941, Henry R. Luce, publisher of both *Time* and *Life* magazines, wrote an editorial predicting that the decades ahead would be an American century, with respect to both the nation's political influence and its economic influence. The nineteenth century had been a British century, a century in which British economic and political influence spanned the globe and it was said that the sun never set on the British Empire (Luce 1941).

Luce's vision was not contradicted by subsequent developments. Unlike Western Europe, the U.S. mainland was spared from bomber attacks and the destruction of its industrial base. Consequently, while in 1950 per capita income in Western Europe stayed at its prewar level, in the United States it was nearly 50 percent above its 1939 level. In 1950, with only 7 percent of the world's population, the United States produced 25 percent of the world's GNP (Maddison 2006).

Despite the high performance of its economy between 1940 and 1950, there was a widespread belief that America was going to return to the massive unemployment levels of the Great Depression. That foreboding was particularly intense in 1943 and 1944 in anticipation of the demobilization of over 11 million soldiers from the armed forces and some 9 million or more workers in defense industries who were simultaneously being let go. So there were about 21 million people about to be thrown into a job market of about 60 million, including the armed forces and the defense establishment (U.S. Bureau of the Census 1955, table 220).

But, as it turned out, the recession of 1945 lasted only eight months and was followed by a robust expansion that lasted thirty-seven months. Moreover, the recession of 1949–50 lasted only eleven months and was followed by another robust expansion that lasted forty-five months. The peak came in 1953 after the economy had already absorbed 20 million potentially unemployed workers, and unemployment was below 3 percent by 1953. Total civilian employment was up by 15 percent over the wartime peak (U.S. Bureau of the Census 2003, table 771; cf. Bratt 1953).

Nevertheless, concern over a return to massive unemployment continued into the 1960s and was strong in the 1970s and 1980s. Although unemployment exceeded 5 percent during some of the years of the long 106-month Kennedy-Johnson expansion, it dropped to 3.5 percent in 1969. Yet, even a quarter of a century after the war, there were still economists (Kuznets 1971a; Maddison 1995; Crafts and Toniolo 1996) who believed that the United States could not have an economy with both growth and low unemployment unless there was a very big government sector. This belief persisted despite much contrary evidence. The United States and other rich countries were well into the post–World War II expansion, the golden age, with growth rates twice the long-term average of the other world leaders. Measured by per capita income, the long-term average growth rate was about 1.9 percent per annum, but the growth rate during the golden age was, for Western Europe, about 3.8 percent. Over the whole period 1950–99, growth rates for GDP averaged between 3.3 and 3.4 percent in Western Europe and the United States.

The wide-ranging debates over the causes of the accelerated growth rates of the golden age suggested some points of consensus. These included the reduction of barriers to international trade, successful macroeconomic policies, and opportunities for catch-up growth following the end of World War II, especially in France, Germany, and Italy. The destruction of much of the prewar capital stock, the reconstruction aid that rebuilt industry with more advanced technology, the successes of macroeconomic policy, the elasticity of the labor supply, high levels of education, and the weakness of vested interests have all been advanced as explanatory factors (Abramovitz 1990; Mills and Crafts 2000; Crafts and Toniolo 1996; Denision 1967; Maddison 1987, 1991, 1995; Olson 1982).

The eventual fading away of the stagnation thesis, of the notion that there was something in the operation of capitalistic economies that made them inherently unstable, brought to the fore several new concerns. These included the growing gap in income between developed and less-developed nations and a new emphasis on cultural and ideological barriers to economic growth in poor countries. In contrast to some of the early theories that suggest that poor countries would grow rapidly if there were large injections of capital from rich countries, by the 1960s the emphasis was that the export of capital would fail to promote growth unless the deep cultural barriers that made these countries unreceptive to the conditions needed for economic growth were somehow overcome. Some commentators, most notably the Nobel Laureate Gunnar Myrdal, said that India would have difficulty sustaining high growth rates because it promoted asceticism and thus undermined the acquisitive culture that spurred Western Europe (see Myrdal 1968).

There was also a shift from worries about oversaving, which never caught on at certain universities. The concern did not catch on at Chicago or at Columbia. Nor did it catch on at the NBER. Analysts such as Kuznets thought that savings were not a threat to but a necessary condition for economic growth because savings were needed both to build infrastructure in developing countries and to get a thriving public sector growing (Kuznets 1961a; Colm 1962; Paul Samuelson, in discussion with the Fogels, 1992).

There was, about this time, a new emphasis on export-led growth. The practice of poor countries selling their exports to rich countries got a bad name during the interwar period and was widely viewed as exploitation of these countries by imperial powers. The later view, looking at the Canadian and American experiences, was quite the contrary. Selling raw materials and other labor-intensive products to the rest of the world is a way to get capital and entrepreneurship from the developed countries to provide those same talents and qualities to the less-developed countries. Thus, at the outbreak of World War I, foreign capital owned one-third of the bonds of American railroads (North 1966; Colm 1962; Ripley 1915; Paul Samuelson, in discussion with the Fogels, 1992).

One of the great discoveries of economic historians during the 1960s—which was confirmed in the 1980s and 1990s—was that the thesis that English coupon clippers got rich from investments in poor countries such as India and then withdrew large sums of annual earnings was wrong. After the computer revolution, it was possible to put the whole late nineteenth-century portfolio of British overseas investments into machine-readable form. It turned out there was a strong correlation between a country's per capita income and the share of the British overseas portfolio invested in it. The United States received the largest share, followed by Canada and Argentina (which at the turn of the twentieth century had one of the highest per capita incomes in the world). Of course, that did not stop die-hard critics of Western imperialism, who denounced Britain for *failing* to have invested in more underdeveloped nations (Simon 1970; Davis and Huttenback 1986; Stone 1999).

There was also about this time (the late 1960s and early 1970s) a new concern about rapid population growth smothering the potential for economic growth in the less-developed countries. It reached the peak with the warning in *The Limits to Growth* (Meadows, Meadows, Randers, and Behrens 1972) of the Club of Rome, which, like Malthus, envisaged that the world population was getting so large so quickly that it would soon outrun global capacity. That was not a view shared by demographers since they believed that, with a lag of about twenty or so years, the fertility rate would follow the death rate down. The world would reach a low-level rate of population increase at low levels of the death rate and birth rate in the same way that there had been low-level growth at high birth and death rates. An acceleration in the growth of the world's population was a transitory phenomenon, owing to the lag in the decline of the birth rate behind the death rate. This forecast became known as the "theory of the demographic transition."

Within two decades, there were many countries with total fertility rates below replacement. Of course, Kuznets never worried about excessive population growth in the West; indeed, he argued that a condition for modern economic growth was that the rise in per capita income had to be accompanied by an increase in population. That was one of his central tenets in his 1966 *Modern Economic Growth*, and he repeated it again in his Nobel address (Kuznets 1971b).

A related concern with the world population taking off in an unprecedented way (with population doubling in less than half a century) was the belief that the production of food could not keep up, and in 2013 we are worried about the global epidemic of obesity. One of the countries that was supposed to be starving was China, which increased its per capita food supply by over 70 percent in four decades. For the world as a whole, calories per capita have grown by 24 percent during the same period, despite the doubling of the population (Fogel 2005).

As remarkable as what was widely forecast in the post–World War II years were the things not foreseen in the 1940s, the 1950s, or even the early 1960s. One of these was the extraordinary economic growth in Southeast and East Asia, beginning first with Japan, which in four decades went from a poor, defeated country to the second largest economy in the world, increasing per capita income tenfold. This was a feat that took leaders of the industrial revolution about 150 years to accomplish. The economic miracle of the high-performing Asian economies other than Japan was also unforeseen, and that state of mind persisted into the 1970s. It was not that economists did not know that per capita income was rising in such countries as Singapore, South Korea, Taiwan, and China. There was, however, a widespread opinion that it could not last, that somehow it was a fluke.

4 :: The Use of National Income Accounting to Study Comparative Economic Growth

It did not require the invention of national income accounting to demonstrate that the United States was becoming increasingly well-to-do. The expansion of the United States geographically from its original location between the Alleghany mountain range and the Atlantic Ocean to a continental power was obvious. And the growth of the U.S. population from just a few million at the time of the Revolution to more than 100 million people early in the twentieth century was also obvious.

Nor did the numerous technological innovations, which drove the American economy and society forward and transformed American culture, escape notice. Indeed, the commissioner of the 1850 census waxed lyrically as he recounted the technological advances of the previous decade: the vast expansion of the railroad system, the fleet of steamboats that plied our inland waterways, the rapid spread of the telegraph network, and the growth of large-scale plants manufacturing cotton textiles and iron. These technological advances were so remarkable, he concluded, that they could not be matched again in the next decade.

A similar theme was struck by the commissioner of the 1900 census, who reviewed the progress of the preceding half century, which included the laying of the Atlantic cable, electric lights, shortwave radio, automobiles based on internal-combustion engines, the completion of the national railroad network, elevators, typewriters, photographic film, diesel engines, fountain pens, the gramophone, escalators, and motion pictures. He also believed that this collection of advances was so spectacular that it could not be repeated in the twentieth century.

During the decade following World War II, when Simon Kuznets began to lay out his research agenda for studying and explaining the high, long-term rates of economic growth, he was aware of the persistent tendency of keen observers to underestimate the capacity for continuing technological advances. Half a century after the dire forecasts of stagnation, technological advances not only continued but likely had also accelerated. Developments in urban sanitation and food processing and the substitution of automobiles for horse-drawn vehicles had led to dramatic declines in the prevalence of deadly infectious diseases. Vaccines, penicillin, and other powerful medicines were widely available to deal with once-fatal diseases. The country had been largely electrified, and a host of household appliances was available to improve the efficiency of home production (refrigerators, washing machines, vacuum cleaners) and to provide low-cost entertainment (radios, phonographs, televisions).

In the election of 1928, Herbert Hoover had made the extravagant promise that, if he was elected president, there would be a chicken (the most expensive meat at the time) in every pot and an automobile in every garage. Yet, by 1955, advances in animal feeds had turned chicken into the cheapest meat, and there were about as many cars as households.

Nevertheless, in the 1950s, the specter of the Great Depression still haunted economists and policymakers, who worried that the postwar boom would peter out, like air escaping from a balloon, and the country would be returned to the clutches of secular stagnation. That fear was not cast out of professional and public discourse during the 1950s. The topic continued to be vigorously debated into the 1960s and beyond.

As early as 1949, Kuznets was one of a relatively few economists who thought that the Great Depression was the exception and that strong, long-term growth was the rule. What was needed was not another (more optimistic) speculative theory to confront the plethora of pessimistic theories but a careful study of history that might yield an empirically warranted theory.

But how to proceed? How to organize research into long-term trends of economic growth? One issue was the unit of observation. Should it be individual entrepreneurs? Climate zones? Ethnic subgroups? Economic social classes? Religious denominations? Kuznets rejected all these options in favor of the nation-state because the available data were organized and maintained by sovereign states. Moreover, he believed that the political system governing the operation of a particular nation-state might turn out to be an important variable in explaining economic growth.

Kuznets's plan to use national income measures to describe and explain the long-term economic trends of the industrial nations was formulated in the late 1930s. However, the execution of that plan was delayed by U.S. involvement in World War II and Kuznets's duties as the chief statistician at the War Production Board. In September 1943, when it was clear that peak wartime production goals had been attained and planning had turned to the transition back to a peacetime economy, Kuznets wrote to Wesley Mitchell, laying out his research plans for after his return to civilian life.

Mitchell was not enamored of a project that aimed to quantify the similarities and differences in the long-term growth patterns of a score of industrialized nations. He doubted the reliability of the data available for most of these nations and urged Kuznets to continue his prior emphasis on trends in the U.S. economy.

Mitchell's unwillingness to have the bureau sponsor his project, which Burns later rejected out of hand, led Kuznets to seek other auspices. This he found at the Social Science Research Council (SSRC) with funding supplied by the Rockefeller Foundation. Although the shift to the SSRC took place in 1949, Kuznets continued to work at the bureau to complete the projects under his supervision that were still in progress (de Rouvray 2004). These included a book presenting estimates of U.S. wealth, national product, and capital formation going back to 1880 (Kuznets 1961a) and his supervision of a series of monographs dealing with long-term trends in capital formation in various sectors of the U.S. economy (for an overview, see Jorgenson 1991). Kuznets's final task for the bureau was a monograph that integrated the various sectoral studies into an integrated overview of the marshaling of capital for economic growth: *Capital in the American Economy* (Kuznets 1961a). With his obligations to the NBER complete, he turned to his project on comparative long-term growth.

Kuznets set out to gather statistics on the growth of nations over a period of at least a half century in order to have secular trends dominate short-term cycles. The data had to be capable of being decomposed in various ways (such as economic sectors and subsectors) in order to study structural changes in the economy during the course of economic growth. The demands of the data meant that his study of growth would be focused on the score or so of nations that had achieved high levels of industrialization by the mid-twentieth century. He characterized the modern industrial system as one in which entrepreneurs applied the empirical findings of science to the solution of problems and the organization of production.

Ten Monographs on Quantitative Aspects of Economic Growth

This research agenda guided Kuznets as he produced ten monographs that were published as supplements to the journal *Economic Development and Cultural Change* under the general title "Quantitative Aspects of the Economic Growth of Nations." The first of these monographs (Kuznets 1956) brought together data on the growth of national product and its components, of populations, and of per capita growth for nineteen nations during the first half of the twentieth century. The text revolved around the discussion of thirty-one very detailed tables. The collection of the data involved efforts of Herculean proportions, and the analysis of the information in the tables was probing and insightful. Kuznets sought to explain the wide variations in the growth rates of per capita income, from a low of 5.6 percent per decade for Spain to a high of 29.2 percent per decade for Sweden (which means that, in half a century, Sweden's per capita income quadrupled while Spain's increased by only 30 percent).

After carefully pointing out various problems and limitations in the assembled data, Kuznets discussed a number of findings that transcended their limitations. One was the deceleration in growth rates after World War I—not only among the losers but also among the winners—which he attributed to institutional destabilizations produced by the war. Another finding was that high rates of population growth did not undermine the growth of per capita income, as some neo-Malthusians believed. Quite the contrary: the available data indicated that high rates of growth in per capita income were positively related to population growth, although the sample size was not large enough to establish statistical significance.

The second monograph in the "Quantitative Methods" series was subtitled "Industrial Distribution of National Product and Labor Force" (see Kuznets 1957). Here, Kuznets sought to characterize differences in the industrial structure of rich and poor nations in the late 1940s. This portion of the monograph series relied on data collected by the United Nations. Kuznets was able to describe long-term changes in the industrial structure of twenty-eight countries, going back a whole century in two of the countries and between half and three-quarters of a century in most of the others.

For purposes of analysis, Kuznets sometimes divided the economy into twelve sectors and sometimes compressed those sectors into three, that he identified as A (agriculture, forestry, and fishing), M (manufacturing, mining, and construction), and S (transportation, communications, commerce, public utilities, government, and other services). His analyses of both the cross-sectional data and trends over time revealed that, as countries got rich, the agricultural share of the labor force declined. Since the output of agriculture increased more rapidly than population and the share of the labor force in agriculture declined, labor productivity in agriculture was rising. Indeed, rising labor productivity in agriculture was necessary to have the labor shares of the M and S sectors rise as rapidly as they did. However, during the first half of the twentieth century, the rate of growth of labor productivity among developed nations was generally much more rapid in the M and S sectors than in the A sector. In general, the shift in the structure of the labor force from agriculture to higher-productivity sectors by itself accounted for about one-fifth of the overall growth in labor productivity, and the remainder was due to productivity growth within each sector.

This monograph was not the first time that Kuznets had shown the relative importance of intersectoral shifts in total economic growth. But never before had he or any other scholar applied this analysis to so many countries over such a long stretch of time.

Kuznets devoted two subsequent entries in the monograph series (Kuznets 1960, 1961b) to the contribution of capital formation to economic growth. One of his principal findings was that rich countries saved more than poor countries (both in cross section for recent years and over time). Moreover, as countries became rich, saving shifted from being concentrated in households to being concentrated in businesses and governments. Surprisingly, the association between savings rates and the growth rates of nations was highly variable, which led Kuznets to conclude that the intensity of capital utilization was more important than sheer accumulation.

The seventh entry in the series (Kuznets 1962) dealt with the share and composition of national product. Kuznets found that, in eleven countries, the household share of consumption was declining while government consumption was on the rise. He also found that, although the share of GDP spent on consumption tended to decline with the rise of per capita income, that decline was limited because changes in technology promoted demand for new goods that satisfied new wants. Consumption was also promoted by the decrease in the inequality of the income distribution.

The eighth entry in the series (Kuznets 1963) reported that the distribution of income in the 1950s was more equal in rich countries than in poor countries. It also reported that inequality of income distribution had narrowed over time, but this narrowing had not generally occurred until after World War I.

The last two monographs in the series (Kuznets 1964, 1967) dealt with the level and structure of foreign trade. From the late nineteenth century to World War I, the foreign trade of most developed countries expanded more rapidly than per capita income. Although this process ground to a halt during the Great Depression of the 1930s, it resumed after the close of World War II. Most of international trade between 1870 and the 1960s was accounted for by Western Europe, the United States, Canada, and Japan either trading among themselves or with underdeveloped countries. Trade purely among underdeveloped countries was minuscule.

Kuznets's Theory of Modern Economic Growth

It is worth noting that the first of these monographs was published in 1956 and the last in 1967. Their order reflected Kuznets's notion of the building blocks on which an empirically based theory of economic growth had to be constructed. Although the monographs contained inklings of the shape of that theory, they were focused on the difficulties in amassing the data for the ultimate analysis and on various shortcomings in those data that needed to be taken into account when generalizing from them.

In 1966, Kuznets published his magnum opus, *Modern Economic Growth*. Although it drew heavily on the statistical data amassed in the ten *Economic Development and Cultural Change* monographs, it was a much more contemplative study. In thinking about the meaning of it all, Kuznets pondered the economic epochs of human history and epochal innovations. By the term *epoch*, he meant a long period possessing distinctive characteristics that gave the period unity and also differentiated it from past or future periods.

By *epochal innovations*, Kuznets meant not only major advances in technology that provided the essential basis for rapid economic growth but also changes in society and human institutions that are conducive to the exploitation of the new technology. It was the interplay of technological and institutional changes that was the essence of modern economic growth, growth that was both rapid and sustained.

The epochal innovation of the era of modern economic growth was the application of science to problems of production. The modern epoch of economic growth was, therefore, the scientific epoch. However, the application of science to production required not only institutional changes but also spiritual changes that were conducive to the flourishing of science. Kuznets characterized these spiritual changes with three terms: *secularism*, *egalitarianism*, and *nationalism*.

By *secularism*, Kuznets meant a concentration on life on earth rather than a focus on heaven. By *egalitarianism*, he meant a denial of inborn differences, except as they manifested themselves in human performance, and recognition that every person was a full-fledged participant in the community of people; there was no hereditary minority entitled by birth alone to a share of economic output. By *nationalism*, he meant a community of feeling, based on history and culture, that tied individuals to other people within the community more tightly together than to people outside the community.

Kuznets went on to list fourteen characteristics of modern economic growth:

1. High rates of per capita growth accompanied by population growth led, in combination, to an enormous increase in total output in the developed nations.

2. The rise in output per capita was due mainly (80 percent) to increased economic efficiency.

3. These improvements in efficiency were particularly striking in commodity production, transportation, and communications.

4. Differential rates of technological advances contributed to the substantial changes in the distribution of output across the main production sectors of the economy.

5. Changes in the structure of output also reflected changes in the structure of demand as income increased.

6. The change in economic structure—particularly the shift away from agriculture, where small firms predominated—led to a significant increase in the scale of firms and a marked rise in the share of the labor force employed by large firms.

7. The change in the structure of output and industry called for rapid institutional adjustments, including changes in fertility rates and migration patterns, and greater government involvement to limit friction among competing groups of workers and between workers and business leaders.

8. Despite the far-reaching changes in the structure and organization of production, the share of labor and capital in income remained relatively stable, as did the distribution of income across income classes (top 10 percent, next 10 percent, etc.), although there had been some narrowing of inequality. Moreover, because

of the opportunities created by the rise of new industries and occupations, individuals were increasingly able to move up the economic ladder.

9. Despite the enormous rise in the reproducible capital stock per capita, consumption still accounted for the overwhelming proportion of national product. However, there were marked shifts in the structure of household consumption, from food, clothing, and shelter to consumer durables (appliances), health services, recreation, and education.

10. International aspects of economic growth were promoted by the technological revolution in transportation and communication. Technological advances in England spread rapidly to the Continent and to European offshoots overseas. This promoted a gap between the developed nations and the other three-quarters of the world.

11. The relatively unrestricted flow of goods and people between Europe and its offshoots prior to World War I promoted economic growth in both areas and also in European overseas colonies.

12. Between 1825 and World War I, the flow of European capital into overseas offshoots and colonies grew rapidly and helped finance economic growth in the recipient countries.

13. The aftermath of World War I, including global economic depression, led to a decline in international flows, particularly in international migration, but also in the flow of capital and, to some extent, in the trade of goods.

14. The fact that the spread of modern economic growth across nations was sequential, not simultaneous, led to marked shifts in political power across nations, which promoted international strain and conflict.

Kuznets's theory of modern economic growth was highly complex. It was a dynamic model because economic relations changed markedly over time. Hence, a set of factors that promoted economic growth at one period of time could become barriers to economic growth later on. His theory also had complex feedback systems that produced unintended and sometimes undesirable consequences, such as high levels of unemployment in low-tech industries or immigration from the countryside to the cities, which led to overcrowding and severe pressure on urban water supplies and sewage disposal systems.

Despite the various dangers that might thwart economic growth, Kuznets was optimistic about the future. He expected technological advances not only to continue but also to accelerate. The increase in population, together with the increasing share of the population that was highly educated, meant that more individuals would become immersed in scientific and technological research. This pool of talent would be enhanced by a growing efficiency in the manufacturing of traditional products that would release workers to the technologically advanced sectors of the economy. Themes of *Modern Economic Growth* were reprised in Kuznets's Nobel Prize lecture (Kuznets 1971).

In *Modern Economic Growth*, Kuznets realized his goal of an empirically based theory of economic growth that would provide a sound basis for economic policy and smooth the institutional adjustments required by accelerating technological advances. He did not consider his theory the last word since unforeseen advances in science and technology would require continuous modifications of the theory.

What was distinctive about Kuznets's theory was that it was a handmaiden of public policy. This characteristic set it apart from the main body of theoretical modeling, which was stimulated more by intellectual curiosity than by the needs of policymakers. Much of economic theory is too abstract to have immediate practical relevance, although it often provides later foundations for policy-oriented theory.

The last point touches on a second aspect of Kuznets's approach: his concern with the role of long-term factors in the determination of current economic performance. In his view, many current economic opportunities and problems were determined by economic conditions and relations that evolved slowly, often taking many decades to work out. At a time when Keynes declared that "in the long run we are all dead," an aphorism reiterated by many economists not only during the 1930s but also during the 1910s and 1950s, Kuznets continued to call attention to the role of long-term factors that had to be taken into account by policymakers, factors that led him to conclude that the opportunities for returning to high employment levels and rapid economic growth were greater than generally believed.

Current social problems, Kuznets emphasized, are often the result of past growth—the consequence of past desirable attainments that at a later time produce socially undesirable consequences that require remedial policy action. Of his numerous illustrations of this principle, one is particularly cogent: the explosive population growth in the less-developed nations of Asia, Africa, Oceania, and Latin America in the quarter century following World War II. This population explosion threatened to thwart efforts to raise per capita incomes from their dismally low levels because birth rates remained traditionally high while public health policies and improved nutrition cut death rates by more than 50 percent in less than a generation. One obvious solution to the problem was to reduce fertility, yet there was a web of traditional patterns of behavior and beliefs that tended to keep fertility high. Nevertheless, Kuznets believed that properly designed public policies could hasten the social and ideological changes required to reduce fertility and lead these societies to prefer a greater investment in a fewer number of children. Such a program required not only government and private campaigns to disseminate the technology of birth control but also a restructuring of social and economic incentives that would provide rewards for families with fewer children.

Kuznets pointed out that this urgently needed program to reduce fertility would have its negative as well as its positive side. Since it was those in upper income brackets who would respond most rapidly to the new incentives, the immediate impact of a campaign to reduce birth rates would be to increase the inequality of the income distribution. This initial impact could be overcome by a determined effort to change the social and economic conditions of the lower classes in a way that would promote an interest in smaller families. Yet, as the experience of the United States and other developed nations has shown, the success of the program to curtail fertility is bound, much further down the line, to create a new set of problems, similar to those that are currently at the center of the modern women's movement: the restructuring of society in such a way as to promote equal opportunity for women in all occupational markets.

Economic growth creates social problems because it is profoundly disruptive to traditional values and religious beliefs, to long-standing social and family patterns of organization, and to numerous monopolies of privilege. Despite the fact that modern economic growth has brought with it tremendous increases in longevity and good health, brought to the lower classes standards of living as well as social and economic opportunities previously available only to a tiny minority, and greatly reduced the inequality in the income distribution of developed nations, the social restructuring that it requires has been fiercely resisted—sometimes because of an unwillingness to give up traditional values and ways of life, sometimes because entrenched classes are determined to protect their ancient privileges. Because of the complex responses to change, and because the epoch of modern economic growth was still unfolding, many aspects of the social restructuring that was under way were still obscure and difficult to predict (Kuznets 1966).

As late as 1972, Kuznets felt compelled to point out that, despite the multitude of tentative partial generalizations, cross-sectional studies, and econometric exercises, there was as yet no "tested generalization, significantly specific to permit the quantitative prediction of aggregate growth, or even of changes in the structural parameters in the course of growth" (Kuznets 1972, 58). The difficulty of predicting the future relates to two methodological problems with which Kuznets continually struggled: How long a period of observation is needed to identify the underlying process at work in any specific aspect of economic growth? How can one determine whether such a process, once identified, is sufficiently stable to provide a reliable basis for prediction? These problems are illustrated by an issue of which Kuznets was the preeminent investigator of his age, the interrelation between demographic processes and modern economic growth.

In the early morning of October 15, 1971, Kuznets received a call from the secretary of the Swedish Academy of Science informing him that he was the winner of the Nobel Prize in economics. The award was made in recognition of his empirically based theory of economic growth. Among the achievements that were singled out were the immense amount of data on which the theory was based, the careful delineation of the uses and vulnerabilities of these data, and some of his insightful new findings. Thus, despite Mitchell's grave doubts about the usefulness of a comparative study of the ways in which various rich nations achieved their high growth rates, such a study was not only feasible but also produced a major advance in knowledge, an assessment certified by the Swedish Academy of Science.

The media picked up on the announcement within minutes, and Kuznets was bombarded with questions about his reaction to the award and what he planned to do with the money. After the flood of interviews subsided, he turned his attention to writing the address he was required to make as part of the week-long agenda of activities organized for him and his party (up to ten family members and friends). It was also a hectic time for Edith, who had to buy a formal gown and deal with the many choices laid before her and Simon by the assistant secretary of the Swedish Foreign Ministry, who functioned as their aide-de-camp both before and during their visit to Sweden. There were receptions galore, visits to universities in Stockholm and Uppsala, and both formal and informal talks at several venues.

On the instruction of the Nobel committee for economics, Kuznets prepared an address that summarized the work for which he was receiving the prize. At the same time, his address went beyond his previous work in some respects, reflecting new lines of research that continued to the end of his career, particularly his analysis of the factors that limited the spread of modern economic growth in the less-developed countries. In this connection, he stressed the obstacles to modern economic growth created by rates of population growth so extraordinary that they threatened to overwhelm efforts to modernize economies.

The Role of Population Growth

Few economists of his era investigated the interrelations between economic growth and population growth as fully as Kuznets. He was impressed more by the salutary effects of rapid population growth than by its negative effects. The evidence, he noted, indicated no cases prior to 1970 in which large increases in population were accompanied by declines in per capita income. Rapid population growth tended to increase per capita income because it increased the number of contributors to useful knowledge. It tended to increase savings because it both increased the ratio of savers to dissavers and increased the amounts saved by upper income groups. Larger populations also promoted economies of scale and responsiveness to new products (because of changes in the age structure of the population). Despite these generally positive aspects of high rates of population growth, Kuznets recognized that the sharp acceleration in the populations of less-developed nations, generally brought about by sharp declines in death rates, sometimes overwhelmed the economies and impeded growth in per capita income.

Kuznets pointed out the economic significance of the fact that accelerated population growth was due primarily to a decline in death rates. The associated decline in morbidity rates served to increase labor productivity, to increase the payoff on the investment in raising and educating children, and to improve the quality of life.

Moreover, the more rapid decline of death rates in cities than in rural areas promoted urbanization and speeded industrialization. The tendency of declining death rates to induce lower fertility rates and promote migration also contributed to economic growth by adapting social institutions to new economic opportunities. The reduction in completed family size and the fact that this occurred at differential rates in rural and urban areas led to a removal of younger generations from the influence of the family and exposed them to modern ethics that promoted participation in a rapidly changing economic system. Kuznets saw this break between ties of blood and economic rewards as a central factor in the victory of objective tests of economic performance over the more traditional rewards given to family connections.

Kuznets's investigations of the synergism between economic change and demographic change were multifaceted. One of his most influential lines of study pertained to the impact of demographic factors on the measured inequality of the distribution of income. Early in his career, Kuznets began to struggle with problems of how to measure the degree of inequality in the distribution of income and how to identify the factors contributing to the inequality. Such decomposition would point to policies that could relieve the appalling economic conditions of the poor that prevailed in all countries at the beginning of the twentieth century. Kuznets believed that, unless the poor shared in the benefits of economic growth at least as fully as the more well-to-do, the stability of society was at risk. He regarded rapid economic growth and greater distributional equality as desirable and generally consistent goals.

During the 1960s and 1970s, when it was apparent that a number of Asian nations had entered onto the paths of both rapid population growth (owing to rapidly declining mortality) and rapid growth in per capita income, some of the available evidence seemed to indicate that these developments were increasing the inequality of the income distribution and hence vitiating the benefits of the modernization of these countries for the poor. Studying the evidence on which this conclusion was based, Kuznets noted that the mechanical application of procedures used for the United States and other developed nations was inappropriate in the Asian context because those procedures failed to take account of the differences in institutions. A key point related to the nature of Asian family cultures, which were different from Western family cultures. As a consequence, the variance in the size of the Asian family (or household) was much larger than in that of the U.S. or Western European family. Not only were the household arrangements of the extended family different, but intrafamily income flows were also different, and these differences were not reflected in standard measures of household income.

When these differences were explicitly acknowledged, a number of important statistical relations emerged. For example, there was a negative correlation between the number of persons per family and the per capita income of families. Consequently, the very identity of the lower and upper income groups changed, depending on whether the size distribution of income was measured by the total income per household or by the average income per person in the household. Moreover, the rate of population growth changed the age structure of households. Countries with rapidly growing populations and high fertility rates had a higher proportion of younger household heads and lower shares of heads over age sixty-five than countries with low population growth. Such demographic variations might increase inequality measured in cross section, even though lifetime income distributions were relatively equal. All these issues could be adequately addressed, Kuznets pointed out, if the sample surveys were designed on the basis of an appropriate theory of the impact of demographic factors on income distributions.

Population Growth as a Propellant of Technological Change

In the 1960s and 1970s, most scholarly opinion held that, even in developed nations, rising population was a severe threat to the continued growth of per capita income. Kuznets strongly dissented from this proposition, arguing that, in modern times, the empirical evidence from developed nations indicated that growth in population accompanied high rates of growth in per capita income. What, then, was the process that prevented output per capita from declining as population pressed against existing resources?

Kuznets stressed three factors. First, labor productivity increased as the labor force grew because there were a variety of unexploited natural resources that were available, and this, combined with a more specialized division of labor, would lead to greater productivity of labor.

Second, when the increase in population was due to a high fertility rate (rather than to immigration or a declining death rate), rates of increase were assisted by internal migration from areas of lower per capita income (rural places) to areas of higher per capita income (the cities). Mobility was important because it permitted a supply of labor to the new industries promoted by technological change. In this connection, young workers were more adaptable to the needs of new industries than older workers, who, because of ingrained habits, were more resistant to change.

Third, because the younger people were better educated than their elders, the absolute number, and probably also the proportion, of gifted contributors to new knowledge would increase. But, even if the proportion of geniuses and other gifted individuals remained constant, the increase in the absolute number of such people would accelerate the advance of knowledge because creative efforts flourished in a dense intellectual atmosphere where many people addressed particular problems and could easily interact with each other with regard to their findings. It was no accident, Kuznets said, that the locus of intellectual progress had been preponderantly in large cities rather than in the thinly settled countryside. There was, he concluded, an interdependence of knowledge among the various parts of the economy and society. Thus, a greater knowledge in chemistry contributes to a greater knowledge of physics, and progress in both fields advances scientific knowledge in physiology and biology.

Kuznets also argued that, in rich countries, population growth increased the investment in human capital, especially when the population growth was due to a decline in the death rate, because then the return on the investment in the education of children increased. Moreover, the expectation of a future in which larger markets and wider opportunities would prevail encouraged the extension of capacity, both personal and material. Such a buoyancy promoted investment in new products and other forward-looking endeavors.

It is now a half century since Kuznets made these forecasts. How well have they held up? In the U.S. case, the answer is, quite well. The U.S. population has increased by two-thirds, and per capita income has tripled. Kuznets was right, and the pessimists were wrong.

Kuznets and Theory

Was Kuznets an economic theorist? Some prominent economic theorists said, Not really. They recognized him as outstanding for his work in the study of business cycles and for his measurement of GDP and inequality. Although they acknowledged that his early work on human capital and on some other issues were contributions to theory, the sum total of these contributions was, they said, modest.

This view was not embraced by the Swedish Academy of Sciences, which awarded Kuznets the Nobel Prize for his elaboration of an empirically derived theory of economic growth. It distinguished his approach to theory from abstract theories that had little bearing on how economies actually worked (Ohlin 1971).

The evolution of economics over the past half century has introduced a dubious equation of economic theory with mathematical models of economic behavior. The confusion between models and theory is unfortunate. Fifty years ago, it was common to call courses in economic theory *economic theory* and to call courses that dealt with mathematical models of economic behavior *mathematical economics*. In the 1950s and 1960s, a course in economic theory was presumed to summarize the body of generalizations about the operation of the economy that economists thought were usually valid. Such generalizations were the core of the basic theory course, even though interesting but controversial generalizations were also presented. In the assessment of economic theories, emphasis was placed not on their intellectual elegance, much as that might be admired, but on their empirical validity.

In the late 1950s and early 1960s, it was not necessary to emphasize that history was one of the principal sources of generalizations about the economy. The contribution of historical knowledge was evident not only from the way in which theory was taught but also from courses in the history of economic doctrine. After all, most of the great theorists between Adam Smith and John Maynard Keynes relied heavily on historical information in propounding their theories. This reliance was evident not only in the work of such verbal theorists as Smith, Thomas R. Malthus, John Stuart Mill, Karl Marx, Thorstein Veblen, J. B. Clark, and Wesley C. Mitchell but also in the work of those economists who were more versed in mathematics, such as Augustin Cournot, W. Stanley Jevons, Alfred Marshall, and Irving Fisher.

It may seem odd to younger economists that a theorist of Joseph A. Schumpeter's stature would have argued, as he did, that economic history was the most essential foundation of a sound training in economics. Schumpeter used the term *economic history* to include not only past but also present-day facts. It was not merely the need of theorists to be versed in facts that led him to make economic history primary. To theorize adequately about economies, he insisted, one had to recognize that "the subject matter of economics is essentially a unique process in historic time." This point implied not only that the economic system was evolving over time but also that recognition of the institutional aspects of economies at particular points in time was essential to good economic analysis. The critical institutions that had to be taken into account were not, in his view, purely economic. Economic history, he argued, afforded the "best method for understanding" how economic and noneconomic institutions "are related to one another and how the various social sciences *should* be related to one another" (Schumpeter 1954, 13).

Emphasizing the role of historical knowledge in the formulation of models does not imply that models—either those formulated mathematically or those formulated verbally—were absent from reasoning about economic behavior until the middle of the twentieth century. After all, Malthus used a very simple mathematical model in his theory of population, and Charles Davenant, Cournot, and Jevons had already formulated mathematical demand curves before Marshall so thoroughly investigated their properties within the context of a simultaneous equation system.[1] See also Fogel (1992); Jevons (1970); and Slicher von Bath (1963). For more on the influence of Cournot, see Creedy (1992), Debreu (1984), and Neihans (1990). Verbal models could be as abstract as mathematical ones, a point that Eugen von Böhm-Bawerk demonstrated with his stories about Robinson Crusoe (see Böhm-Bawerk 1890). Of course, whether verbal or mathematical, these abstract models were presumed to be not an end in themselves but a basis for arriving at valid generalizations about how some aspect of the economy actually worked.[2]

---

1. Davenant's curve, also called King's law, was represented arithmetically but is

$$Q = P^{-0.403}.$$

2. Economists sometimes tend to equate theory with generalizations that involve cause-and-effect statements. These are a very important subclass of theories, especially if one wants to probe the empirical validity of counterfactual conditional statements (e.g., Fogel 1964; Fogel and Engerman 1969). However, some theories are purely descriptive. Perhaps the most famous is the Darwinian theory of evolution, which will not support counterfactual conditional statements (cf. Blaug 1980; and Lewontin 1970). However, even statements that will support counterfactuals are also descriptions because they purport to describe how one or more variables will change as other variables change (cf. Fogel 1970). On laws and lawlike sentiments in history, see Joynt and Rescher (1961). On counterfactuals and causal statements, see Simon and Rescher (1966) and Rescher (1971).

The last point needs to be emphasized. Mathematical models are not generalizations about the economy. They are, as the word *model* implies, an abstract representation, which in engineering, physics, and chemistry is sometimes constructed in relief from clay and at other times constructed in plastic or some other material to represent a variety of surfaces and objects. In economics, models are often mathematical analogies that serve to represent in a simplified way some aspect of economic behavior. Analyzing the properties of a mathematical model is not the same thing as analyzing the way in which the economy actually works. Indeed, the properties of equilibrium in the real world do not depend, as they do in some models, on whether the number of markets is odd or even. As Lionel W. McKenzie said to Bob Fogel in conversation in the early 1960s when he and other mathematical economists were struggling to prove the existence and uniqueness of an equilibrium within a Walrasian model: "We know that equilibria exist because markets produce them every day. The problem is that we ran into difficulties in demonstrating their existence in our models."

Economists study the properties of models because experience has shown that doing so yields useful, sometimes powerful analytic tools that help explain how the economy actually works. For example, linear programming, a mathematical procedure developed shortly after World War II as a planning instrument for the U.S. Air Force, turned out to be a powerful addition to economic analysis. One important aspect of programming is the concept of duality: for every primal problem in which the inputs of labor and capital are combined to maximize output, there is a dual problem in which the shadow prices of these inputs are chosen to minimize their costs. The two solutions are equal. The concept of duality, carried over to production theory, made it possible for economic historians and other empirical students of economic growth to circumvent the paucity of data on physical inputs and outputs by using the relatively abundant data on prices to estimate technological change in various industries going back as far as 1600.

Another virtue of mathematical modeling is that it frequently makes apparent not only logical errors but also empirical errors and unwarranted conclusions that beset more informal types of reasoning. Robert M. Solow showed that the widespread belief of the late 1940s and early 1950s that physical capital formation was the key to economic growth stemmed from the assumption that the capital-output ratio and the savings rate were fixed. Using a more flexible production function, he demonstrated empirically that, in a model with two or more variable inputs, changes in the amount of physical capital (per se) explained only a small part of the record of U.S. economic growth.[3]

Thus, history and mathematical models are two productive, often complementary ways of searching for valid generalizations about the economy. Another case in point is Douglass C. North's use of the price dual in production theory to demonstrate his discovery that most of the productivity gains in ocean shipping between 1600 and 1850 were due not to new technologies but to institutional changes: the elimination of piracy changed the distribution of preexisting ships crossing the Atlantic, permitting large, lightly armed vessels with high carrying capacity and low costs to become predominant (North 1968).

Although the application of the duality theorem provided more precision, it was North's historical research that led to the discovery that the elimination of piracy was crucial to the improvement in productivity. This striking discovery brought new attention to the key role played by the institutional context in influencing the rate of the diffusion of existing technologies. So it is the substance of the findings, not infatuation with the methods, that is crucial in producing valid theoretical generalizations. Neither the elegance of a mathematical model nor the beauty of a literary passage in economic history by itself guarantees that the generalizations derived from each of these sources is useful in giving guidance to policymakers.

3. One other point worth making about mathematical models pertains to empirical tests of the validity of a theory. Whether the theory comes from a mathematical model or from a study of history, it is often necessary to formulate some aspect of the theory mathematically in order to measure the key variables of the theory or to estimate key parameters. Measurement also involves modeling, although the models used to test or explore the range of applicability of a particular theory might be quite different from the mathematical model that produced the generalization to which we apply the epithet *theory*. See Solow (1957).

We have stressed Kuznets's theoretical generalizations not because we consider all of them to have been validated empirically but because so many of them are still central to theoretical discussion about economic growth, for both the developed countries and the developing countries. By contrast, *some* of the generalizations derived from the mathematical modeling of economic growth, such as the implications of "putty-clay models," ceased to be of interest shortly after they were put forward, despite the initial enthusiasm for them.

Kuznets's work has much in common with the work of Schumpeter and Theodore W. Schultz. Schumpeter was the most important growth theorist between the deaths of Smith and Malthus and his own death in 1950. His earlier work focused on long cycles in economic output, which he attributed to fluctuations in the rate of inventions and innovations. His analysis led him to single out entrepreneurs as the dynamic agents of change, to point to the equity effects of economic growth (embodied in his concept of "creative destruction"), and to make the creative clusters of innovations inherently inflationary.[4] It is the late Schumpeter, however, rather than the early one, who is closest to North's concerns. The late Schumpeter focused on the conflict between the capitalist system of economic organization and the political, social, and intellectual movements that were hostile to capitalism for ideological reasons. It was these conflicts, he argued, rather than the secular diminution of investment opportunities that threatened the continuation of economic growth under a system of political democracy (cf. Rostow 1990).

Schultz has received the most acclaim for his contributions to the theory of human capital. But that was only one aspect of his broader concern with economic growth and the elimination of poverty. These broader concerns led him to examine closely the impact of government fiscal policies and specific interventions into agriculture in both developed and developing countries, policies that distorted agricul-

---

4. This arises from Schumpeter's assumption of full employment in his model. If entrepreneurs require credit to finance their innovations, the initial injection of credit into the economy expands the money supply through the multiplier effect. However, since innovation takes time, there is no immediate expansion of output. Hence, in the short run, innovation leads to inflation. If innovation is continuous, inflation will be as well.

tural production and had perverse effects on the distribution of income. Like Schumpeter, Schultz was concerned about new sources of future income growth, and this concern led him to recognize that, in the twentieth century, human capital had become more important than physical capital in explaining both economic growth and the inequality of the income distribution. His theory of human capital led him to conclude that unregulated high fertility was a major factor in destabilizing the agricultural sector. Such considerations also caused him to emphasize the importance of the investment in improving nutrition and health as a key to economic growth in poor nations and to identify investment in "allocative skills" as a key to dealing with problems of disequilibria (cf. Bowman 1980).

Each of these economists was heavily influenced in the formation of his theory by the pressing policy issues of his era. Schumpeter was concerned with the unevenness in secular patterns of growth across nations as well as over time and across classes within nations, an unevenness that created sharp political tensions and promoted international conflicts. Kuznets, during his early years, shared Schumpeter's concerns about the instability of economic growth in particular nations, although he recognized that, after aggregation across the advanced European nations, the secular pattern of growth was much more even. Like Schumpeter, he saw technological change as the engine of economic growth but focused on the unevenness brought about by the life cycle of an innovation, the pattern of population change, and the changes in the demand for output. In his later years, during the exceptional worldwide spurt in economic growth that began early in the 1950s, Kuznets focused on the continuing potential for economic growth and the policies that would do most to promote economic growth in the developing nations.

Schultz was influenced in his thinking about human capital by his experiences with postwar reconstruction. Despite the devastation of Europe, all the war-ravaged countries experienced rapid economic growth in the 1950s, quickly exceeding their prewar levels. This led Schultz to dwell on the key role of human capital in modern economic growth, to consider the possibility that a significant share of the so-called residual factor in economic growth was due to improvements in the quality of the inputs, particularly in the quantity of capital embodied in human labor. Although his empirical work on this question focused on education, he recognized that, theoretically, improvements in health, in the capacity to process information, in the development of allocative skills, and in on-the-job training might be more important than the effects of formal education per se.

5 :: The Scientific Methods of Simon Kuznets

"Anyone can start a row in economics; it is much harder to find out what is really happening to the economy." Simon Kuznets made this statement during a conversation he had with Henry Rosovsky, who was then chairman of the Economics Department at Harvard University and later became dean of the Faculty of Arts and Sciences, and Robert Fogel at Harvard in the early 1970s. Fogel was startled when he said it since their profession thrived on controversy. Indeed, to many economists, cleverness in debate, rather than the applicability of the debate to any issue of the real world, is what economics is all about. To Kuznets, however, there was a real economic world, and the task of the economist was to describe it accurately and to explain it in a way that would be helpful to those who had to make economic policy.[1]

Some Aspects of Kuznets's Approach to Economics

If there was any aspect of Kuznets's approach to economics that may be said to have dominated all the others, it was his concern with the great policy issues of his age. Emphasis on this point may surprise those who are familiar with his work since he never became directly involved in those highly politicized disputes over economic policy that

---

1. For a general introduction to Kuznets's scientific method, see Easterlin (1989), Abramovitz (1971, 1985), Patinkin (1976), Ben-Porath (1986), Bergson (1986), and Bergson, Leibenstein, Rosovsky, and Griliches (1987).

often split the profession into partisan camps. Moreover, many of the problems on which Kuznets worked, such as the relation between the rate of population growth and the rate of technological innovation, are hardly likely to be resolved or even affected significantly by new legislation, nor did his findings on such issues enter prominently into the shifting partisan alignments of his age. Nevertheless, he recognized the importance of the points at issue in the political debates over economic policy, and he believed that the development of a reliable body of evidence bearing on these issues was an urgent task of economists. He saw economics as an empirical science aimed at disclosing the factors that affect economic performance.

It is important to keep in mind how new the issues with which Kuznets grappled during his career were when he first began to address them in the mid-1920s. The proposition that Western Europe and America had undergone an irreversible economic transformation—an industrial revolution—was not effectively enunciated until the end of the 1880s. Although optimism about the economy was widespread during the first three decades of the twentieth century, these years also spawned influential theories that economic progress was grinding to a halt. The notion of a general crisis for capitalism, set forth in the work of such socialist or radical theorists as J. A. Hobson of England, Rudolf Hilferding of Germany, and Vladimir Lenin, became widely accepted by professional economists during the 1930s.[2] Alvin Hansen, in his 1938 presidential address to the American Economic Association, suggested that a correct fiscal policy could bring an end to secular stagnation. Despite a certain optimism, that speech seemed to endorse the view that secular stagnation was the natural condition of free market economies in the twentieth century and that capitalist economies could be kept afloat only with massive government intervention (Hansen 1939; cf. Abramovitz 1952).

When Kuznets first began his work on economic growth in the mid-1920s, not all the processes that he later identified had worked

2. J. A. Hobson (1858–1940) was an English political thinker and a promoter of "New Liberalism." Rudolph Hilferding (1877–1941) was a Marxist theorist and the chief theoretician of the Social Democratic Party of Germany.

themselves out. Europe and America were still passing through their demographic and epidemiological transitions (U.S. life expectancy at birth in 1920 was still under fifty-five years), and the nature of these phenomena was not yet fully apparent. It would be another two decades before the theory of the demographic transition—which explains that declines in the death rate lead, with a lag, to comparable declines in the birth rate—was formulated, and it would be another three to four decades before it became clear that the economic advances of the last half of the nineteenth century were part of a new epoch of economic growth that was about two centuries old and that was in the process of spreading from its origins in Western Europe and in certain countries of European settlement to the impoverished nations of Africa, Asia, and Latin America.

Kuznets considered the acceleration of population growth during the nineteenth century as not only one of the most important consequences of economic growth but also a major factor contributing to it. A particularly important aspect of the phenomenon was the concentration of the decline of death rates at early ages, which contributed to the reduction in fertility rates. The reduced fertility rates released a large proportion of the female labor force to gainful occupations, accelerated the transition to modern families, mobile and responsive to economic incentives, and promoted new ideologies conducive to economic growth (Kuznets 1966, 56–62). In this connection, Kuznets noted the increase in the share of women in the U.S. labor force from 17 percent in 1890 to 27 percent in 1950, which he attributed to the lower fertility rates, the shift in employment opportunities from manual to service-sector positions, and urbanization, which made organized labor markets more accessible to women. He also called attention to the fact that the most rapidly growing occupations—those in the professional, technical, clerical, sales, and other services—were the ones in which women had made the greatest inroads. Nevertheless, in the late 1950s and early 1960s, when the new women's movement was still incipient, he anticipated neither the explosive entry of women into the labor force during the next quarter century nor the new ideology that would facilitate that development (Kuznets 1966, 193–95).

Another aspect of Kuznets's method was his approach to the establishment of the priorities for empirical research in economics. At any moment, there are more issues and problems demanding the attention of economists than there are resources to address them. In Kuznets's view, the priorities for research were determined by a complex interaction of three factors: (1) the needs of policymakers inside and outside the government, particularly, the issues that they considered paramount for promoting economic growth, stability, and equity; (2) the beliefs of economists and other social scientists regarding the most effective measures for resolving the problems on this social agenda; and (3) the availability of the data needed to address these issues and the effectiveness of the tools, both analytic and mechanical, required to process and analyze the data (Kuznets 1972, 39).

In explaining both the enormous growth of economic research between 1930 and 1970 and the direction that research took, Kuznets emphasized the importance of the interaction between these three factors, rather than the ascendency of any one over the other. This expansion of economic research undoubtedly depended on the social agenda since it was largely through the government that the training of the scientific personnel, the collection of the primary data, and the financing of individual research projects were directly or indirectly promoted.[3] However, which direction this research took was heavily influenced by developments within the academic community. Thus, while the devastating impact of the Great Depression of the 1930s promoted greater government intervention in the economy, the direction that the intervention took, and the type of research that the government promoted, was greatly affected by Keynesian theory, which had gained such dominance in the scholarly community. In the absence of this influential theory, government policy "might have been limited to new provisions for unemployment insurance, new plans for public works, and the like" (Kuznets 1972, 42). Since the theory indicated that depression conditions could recur unless the government was continuously concerned with ensuring a sufficiently high level of final demand, government policy moved heavily in a Keynesian direc-

---

3. Foundations and other private institutions also played an important role (Kuznets 1972, 42).

tion. This interaction between social priorities and economic theory gave an enormous stimulus to the development of national income accounts, of measures of employment and unemployment, the size distribution of income, and other macrovariables, as a means of monitoring economic performance and guiding government intervention.

Kuznets emphasized the critical role played by academic research in the innovations in economic measurement adopted by government agencies in the free market economies. It was not primarily from the government bureaucracy but from the scholarly community that new approaches to measuring economic performance arose. It was not until those approaches had been advanced and explored within the scholarly community that the national income and product accounts, input-output analysis, flow-of-funds measures, and periodic sample surveys were adopted by government agencies as standard procedures on which they relied.

An emphasis on the intimate interconnection between measurement and theory was a third, and perhaps the most distinctive, aspect of Kuznets's method. Although Kuznets was a quintessential empiricist and a standard bearer for empirical research, his empiricism did not imply hostility to theory. Quite the contrary, he continually emphasized that a sound theory was needed to identify the variables that had to be measured and that theory had to be invoked in order to determine how the raw data thrown up by normal business or government activities had to be combined in order to create the desired measures. Since measurement was dependent on theory, he emphasized that as theory advanced, owing to either deeper insights or sounder empirical knowledge, past measures would have to be revised. Thus, empirical knowledge and theoretical knowledge are at any point in time only asymptotically valid, subject to changing knowledge in both areas as well as to changing social goals and values (Kuznets 1972, 18–22). In attempting to pursue his empirical objectives, Kuznets frequently encountered theoretical issues that had not yet been addressed adequately. On such occasions, he made notable contributions to theory, as in his work on the theory of national income accounting, in which he extended utility theory to issues involved in designing measures of output that reflected economic welfare.

Kuznets not only used theory but also sought to extend it by identifying empirical regularities that could provide the basis for new theories or by modifying and extending existing ones. In this connection, he made notable contributions to the theory of technological change, the theory of industrialization and other aspects of long-term structural changes in modern economies, the theory of economic cycles, the theory of the size distribution of income, the theory of the interrelation between population change and economic growth, the theory of capital formation (including the role of variations in saving rates over the life cycle), and the theory of the effect of changes in vital statistics on the socioeconomic characteristics of households.

How to Measure in Economics

To many of those who have studied the work of Kuznets, his demonstrations and discussions of the art of measurement are the most valuable aspects of his legacy. By *the art of measurement*, we mean not merely statistical theory and econometric theory, which are important but quite adequately conveyed in papers and books. A far more difficult question in practice is how to apply statistical methods and economic models to the incomplete and biased data with which economists normally work and still produce reliable estimates of key economic variables and parameters. That question cannot be answered by a simple rule because economic data are so variable in quality and because the circumstances under which a given set of defects in the data are tolerable depends on the issues that are being addressed, on the statistical and analytic procedures that are being employed, and on the sensitivity of the results to systematic errors in the data, to the choice of behavioral models, and to the choice of statistical procedures.

Good judgment on these issues is developed with experience, and, both in his writing and in his class lectures, Kuznets tried to convey his rich experience on these matters in the same way that doctors use rounds to teach medical students the art of diagnosing illnesses. Kuznets conducted his "rounds" with his students at Pennsylvania, Johns Hopkins, and Harvard in three different ways: first, in his lectures on economic growth, where he discussed problems of measurement and gave numerous examples of good and bad attempts to measure key economic variables and relations; second, in his seminar on the application of quantitative methods to the analysis of time series, which was largely a laboratory course in which students applied various procedures to typical bodies of economic data and collectively discussed the problems and interpreted the outcomes; third, in his supervision of dissertations, during which he varied his approach according to the degree of independence desired by the student while always serving as a sympathetic, thorough, and penetrating critic.

Kuznets held that, while the statistical analysis of quantitative data was a powerful instrument in the study of long-term changes in the economies of nations, it provided no magical solutions. Quite the contrary, it was filled with pitfalls that had entrapped some of the most able investigators (virtually no one was immune), and, even when the data were good, the procedures appropriate, and the results fairly unambiguous, great care had to be exercised in drawing conclusions about the domain to which the findings applied and the predictions that could reliably be based on them. High on his list of major dangers was the superficial acceptance of primary data without an adequate understanding of the circumstances under which the data were produced. Adequate understanding involved detailed historical knowledge of the changing institutions, conventions, and practices that affected the production of the primary data but were difficult to ascertain and quantify.

Another point high on Kuznets's list of major dangers was the easy assumption that the good fit of a mathematical model to the data made that model an adequate description of the significant features of the data. Because of the limitations of data, especially in time series, many mathematical models, varying in complexity and structure, may give fairly good fits to a given body of data. Nor can Occam's razor (the theory that holds that simpler explanations are preferable to complex ones) be glibly invoked to settle such issues since it is possible that the curve giving the best fit incorrectly leads to the conclusion that the data were generated by a simple process, an elegant "law" of behavior embodied in a single equation, when in fact they were generated by several distinct processes that are badly distorted by the simple function.

Kuznets's comments on methods were always deeply embedded in a more general evaluation of the substantive findings of a particular investigation. Thus, whether a given body of data was good or bad depended not only on the inherent limitations of the data set but also on the types of measures that were being constructed from it and the issues to which these measures were addressed. Consequently, his evaluation of the validity of substantive findings tended less to be cast as simply right or wrong, although this was sometimes the judgment, and more often focused on the reliability of the results (usually expressed as the probable range of error in the estimates).

Although he placed great emphasis on the development of databases of the highest quality (i.e., those least afflicted by sample selection biases, by definitional changes that led to lumping data that are intrinsically different in some important dimension into the same category, etc.), Kuznets was not a purist who insisted on working only with "perfect" data. Since no data set is ever perfect, his emphasis was on how to exploit the data at hand in order to extract from them whatever useful information they might contain. But then the effect of the limitations of the data on the resulting analysis had to be specified, with some results treated as conjectural and still others merely as illustrative computations. Providing that they were carried out with due caution regarding the nature of the results, such preliminary analyses were useful because they increased the likelihood of upgrading the available data sets or closing gaps in them by demonstrating the social usefulness of such efforts. Indeed, Kuznets viewed the preliminary analysis of the available data as an essential part of an asymptotic process of discovery, during which both the underlying data sets and the analytic procedures were perfected and made more suitable to the resolution of the substantive issues.

Like many other statisticians, Kuznets worried about imposing so much structure on the data that the a priori assumptions of the investigation overwhelmed whatever information there was in the data. He was skeptical about fitting simple (two- or three-parameter) curves to data sets with relatively few observations of questionable quality.

Consequently, he tended to work with frequency distributions, usually in either one-way or two-way classifications, rather than with regressions.

Kuznets had numerous horror stories of how very able investigators had been misled by relying too heavily on a priori assumptions of what the world was really like and on arguments by analogy as well as by misplaced confidence in formal measures of goodness of fit. A case in point is his discussion of Raymond Pearl's contention that a simple logistic curve summarized tendencies so stable in human populations that it represented a law of population growth. Pearl, a noted biologist and statistician and the author of *The Biology of Population Growth* (1925), conducted experiments with fruit flies raised in closed containers that show that, with increasing density and a fixed food supply, the growth of the population was well described by a logistic curve (an S-shaped curve that starts off gradually, then rises steeply, then evens out). Using Malthusian types of arguments, he contended that the analogy applied to man because space is also limited on earth. He then proceeded to fit logistic curves to data for various populations and, with one or two exceptions that he explained as special cases, obtained apparently good fits. Pearl also showed that one of the conditions for a logistic curve to be applicable, a decline in birth rates as population density increases, was supported by cross-sectional regressions on U.S. cities between birth rates and two density measures, after controlling for city size and per capita wealth or income. One implication of Pearl's findings was that population growth moved in long cycles, with population increasing until it came close to its asymptote. It hovered at this asymptote until some exogenous factor caused the asymptote to shift.

Kuznets carefully discussed both the a priori and the statistical aspects of the argument, pointing out that, although Pearl gathered the data to test his theories from a fairly exhaustive list of those nations for which such data were available, represented on that list were mainly Western nations at relatively high levels of economic development. The observations were primarily for the period from the early or mid-nineteenth century to 1920, and, since they were usually decennial estimates, there were generally about twelve or fewer observations per country; consequently, good fits in the sense of a high R^2 did not mean that the results were significant. Even if the fits were statistically significant, however, they did not necessarily justify the conclusion that the underlying process was well described by a logistic curve or provide the basis for a law invariant regardless of social and cultural conditions. Since the logistic curve has three segments (convex from above, linear, and concave from above), it would give a good fit to data sets that were strictly linear as well as to those that were strictly increasing at a decreasing rate or strictly increasing at an increasing rate. Examination of the underlying data revealed such segmentation to be pretty much the case.

Kuznets's manner of discussing these examples was nearly as important as the substance of his points. There was no attempt to demean Pearl or to puff up his own image. His aim was to demonstrate both the possibilities and the limitations of quantitative methods in the social sciences. Valuable as they were, such methods did not provide easy, let alone automatic, solutions to otherwise difficult problems. No matter how high-powered the technique, the results it yielded had to be carefully evaluated not only by looking at such internal evidence as the scatter of observations around the fitted curve but also by thoroughly considering such relevant external evidence as the nature of the societies that yielded the data and the conventions followed by the agencies that gathered, processed, and published them.

The results, Kuznets emphasized time and again, had meaning only if the investigator defined and studied the universe from which the data were drawn, and that required a substantial effort to discover and understand the relevant social institutions of the societies under study as well as how they were changing over time. Required to be a good quantitative economist, then, were not only logical and technical cleverness but also a substantial knowledge of recent and more distant history. Although Kuznets admired cleverness and technical proficiency, he considered the capacity to be thorough and to pursue details rigorously as a rarer quality and as a more binding constraint on good work.

In assessing the reliability of particular estimates, Kuznets emphasized the importance of systematically investigating their relation to other series and other kinds of information that were logically related to them. He was, in this connection, a master of devising algebraic identities that brought other available data to bear on the estimates at issue in a particularly illuminating way. These identities were also marvelous devices for revealing implicit and unsupported assumptions and thus contributed to the social research agenda. A dazzling example of this skill is contained in his evaluation of the time series on U.S. national income and its sectoral distribution generated by Robert F. Martin for the period 1799–1869 (Kuznets 1952a, 1952b). What puzzled Kuznets about these widely cited figures was that they implied a decline of about 8 percent in per capita income over the forty years between 1799 and 1839, years that witnessed vigorous growth in population, a vast geographic expansion, and the introduction and initial diffusion of the steamboat, the railroad, and the factory system.

To evaluate Martin's series in the light of the available data, Kuznets employed an identity[4] that related per capita income to wages in agriculture and in the rest of the economy and to the labor force participation rate. Marshaling the available fragments of data, he surmised that, even if there had been no increase in wage rates over the period 1799–1839, the rise in nonagricultural labor relative to agricultural labor, together with the rise in the labor force participation rate, should jointly have led to about a 19 percent increase in per capita income since, as indicated by Martin's data, the ratio of nonagricultural to agricultural wages was equal to about 5. He then went on to marshal fragmentary data suggesting that both agricultural and nonagricultural wages had probably risen, contrary to the implication of Martin's series, so that even Kuznets's own exercise probably underestimated the total growth of per capita income during the period 1799–1839.

This exercise touched off a major stream of research involving numerous investigators that have greatly illuminated the course of U.S.

---

4. The algebraic statement of this identity is

$$\bar{Y} = \rho(\lambda_a W_a + \lambda_n W_n),$$

where $\bar{Y}$ = per capita income, ρ = the labor force participation rate, λ_a = the share of the labor force in agriculture, λ_n = the share of the labor force in nonagriculture, W_a = output per worker in agriculture, and W_n = output per worker in nonagriculture.

economic growth prior to 1840. It was characteristic of Kuznets that he considered the mathematics underlying his computations so obvious that he never made the underlying equation explicit. Although this and other Kuznetsian identities were often used by his students in teaching, the simple equation (or a variant of it) was not put into print until the publication of Paul David's influential paper in 1967 (Engerman and Gallman 1983; David 1967; see also Fogel, Galantine, and Manning 1992; and Fogel and Engerman 1992a, 1992b), more than a decade after Kuznets's original discussion of it. Subsequently, a variety of Kuznetsian and Kuznets-like identities have been set forth as differential equations and effectively exploited.

Did the numerous biases that afflicted the data sets with which economists had to work, the pitfalls of curve fitting, and the sensitivity of results to the presumed underlying behavioral models as well as to the choice of statistical procedures doom the usefulness of quantitative methods in the study of economic growth? By no means. Kuznets was neither an optimist nor a pessimist on this question but a realist and an architect of procedures needed to make the most of defective data and imperfect tools. Even in the most difficult of circumstances, he pointed out, such as those that confronted Pearl in his attempt to demonstrate that the logistic curve represented the law of human population growth, there was important information to be gleaned. What Pearl had indirectly demonstrated was that all the advanced nations for which data were available had experienced declines in their percentage rates of natural increase between 1850 and 1920. That finding was robust no matter what segment of the logistic curve Pearl had fitted to his data since it is a characteristic of the logistic function that the percentage rate of increase is always declining. This was no mean finding. It was one of the early demonstrations of what subsequent research confirmed as a major demographic feature of modern economic growth. Hidden among the oysters was a genuine pearl.

The last point calls attention to what we believe was the most powerful lesson that Kuznets taught about the art of measurement in economics: sensitivity analysis. It was sensitivity analysis, not clever a priori arguments, that separated robust findings from conjectures. Anyone good enough to get a Ph.D. after the mid-1950s could marshal an a priori case for why one procedure should be preferred over another or why some bias in the data could be ignored. It was much harder to demonstrate that a finding based on such a priori arguments should be taken seriously since it was equally easy to construct a priori arguments proving that the designated procedure badly biased the result or that the imperfections in the data were fatal. Kuznets's solution to such problems was *sensitivity analysis,* by which he meant a careful examination of both the procedures and the data in order to see whether plausible ranges of the systematic errors in the data or the substitution of reasonable alternative estimation procedures would make a material difference in the finding. If they did not, the finding was robust; otherwise, the data added nothing to the theoretical considerations that preceded the measurement. The original conjecture was still just a conjecture.

Kuznets as a Theorist

Kuznets is one of the most important theorists since Keynes. Some measure of his impact on theory in one of the major areas of his research, the interrelation between population change and economic growth, is provided by the author index of *The Determinants and Consequences of Population Trends* (United Nations 1973–78). Prepared by a UN commission, the study summarizes and interprets the worldwide literature in this field from the earliest times to the 1970s. Among the individuals frequently cited in the author index are such innovators in demography as Ansley J. Coale, Richard A. Easterlin, Thomas R. Malthus, and the Nobel laureates W. A. Lewis and Gunnar Myrdal. The citations of Kuznets, however, exceed those of any of these specialists, usually by large margins. They even exceed the citations of such collective authors as the Food and Agriculture Organization of the United Nations, the International Labour Organization, the OECD, and the World Health Organization. Indeed, only the combined agencies of the United Nations have more citations than Kuznets.

Since the interrelation between population growth and economic growth is only one of the major themes on which Kuznets theorized, it is possible to present only some brief comments about his approach to theory. In this connection, it is useful to begin with a distinction that he often made between a partial and a general theory of economic growth. By a *partial theory*, he meant the in-depth consideration of a few variables torn from the context of the general process of economic growth. In this connection, he welcomed the explosion of mathematical growth models that began in the late 1940s and the 1950s as a return to issues that had been so important to Smith, Malthus, and Schumpeter, thus finally overcoming the long neglect of growth theory. Yet he feared that, because of the severe aesthetic constraints placed on the issues and on the interrelations of variables by the type of mathematic modeling that was fashionable, this stream of research might rapidly dissipate without making a lasting contribution to what he considered the principal objective of theoretical work in this field: the development of a tested and confirmed general theory of growth that included a theory of technological change, of population growth, of changes in the economic structure of production, of changes in political and social organization, and of the role of international political relations. A general theory needed not only to encompass each of these major elements but also to describe the feedback mechanisms that linked them together in a dynamic context.

Kuznets recognized that such a general theory was a tall order that would probably not be accomplished in his lifetime. He not only welcomed partial models as contributions toward that goal, as long as they contributed to the ultimate object of a general theory; he himself contributed numerous partial models. His presidential address to the American Economic Association, in which he considered the impact of economic growth on the inequality of the income distribution (Kuznets 1955), exemplifies his approach to such partial theories. It was in this paper that he set forth the hypothesis that, in early stages of economic growth (i.e., at low levels of per capita income), growth tended to increase the inequality of the income distribution but that, at later stages (high levels of per capita income), it reduced inequality. That hypothesis, which has come to be known in the literature as the *inverted-U hypothesis* (or the *Kuznets curve*), set off a large train of both theoretical and empirical research aimed at elaborating it and testing it empirically. It has been put to practical use by the World Bank, which transformed the hypothesis into an econometric model suitable for estimating the share of the world population living in poverty (Anand and Kanbur 1984, 1987, 1993; cf. Fei, Ranis, and Kuo 1978).

It is interesting to note that Kuznets's 1955 paper has been treated not only as important theoretically but also as providing empirical support for the inverted-U hypothesis (Fields 1980, 78, 84). This is a strange development since Kuznets was at pains to stress its theoretical nature, repeatedly warning that his allusions to fragmentary data were not evidence but little more than pure guesswork. Most of the paper is devoted to explicating the conflicting factors that arose during the course of growth and created pressures both to increase and to reduce inequality. It also describes processes that influenced the relative strength of the conflicting factors at different stages in the growth process.

It would have been easy for Kuznets to set forth his model in mathematical form (since the computations he presented to illustrate the process implied a set of equations), but he chose to make the same points with numerical examples. Numerical examples had two advantages over a mathematical presentation. They emphasized the limited range of the changes in the key variables and parameters needed to bring about the postulated curve, and they made his argument accessible to a wider range of readers. Since there was nothing in the model that required a long chain of reasoning to reveal some deeply buried implication, there was no reason to unnecessarily restrict his audience.

This example reveals something important both about Kuznets's approach to theory and about certain problems in the profession. Because Kuznets developed a theory consistent with the available fragmentary evidence, because he used numbers rather than algebra to set forth the theory, his paper was widely interpreted as an empirical paper despite his repeated warnings about the fragility of the data suggesting the theory. He also stressed that, even if the data turned out to be valid, they pertained to an extremely limited period of time and to exceptional historical experiences and that caution had therefore to be exercised in the conclusions drawn from his theory.

Nevertheless, his caveats were jettisoned and his hypothesis raised to the level of law, becoming the basis for numerous formal models and elaborate econometric exercises, some of which lost touch with the complex reality that he was trying to uncover and characterize.

The example calls attention to a shortcoming of current theory: the tendency to value a theory according to the type of the mathematics it employs. On this criterion, the best theory employs the most general mathematics, as free as possible from empirical or quasiempirical limitations, as the specification of the form of functions. But that criterion is purely aesthetic—equivalent to constraints that the sonnet form imposes on a poet. Aside from aesthetic considerations, such severe limitations are generally unnecessary in economics because the range of most economic variables is fairly constrained. Making use of that knowledge frequently makes it possible to solve models that cannot be solved in a purely analytic (abstract) framework. Ansley Coale, an elegant analyst, has frequently made use of the limited ranges of variation in demographic behavior to close demographic models with empirical relations and thereby manipulate models that would otherwise remain intractable. It is this flexibility in demographic modeling that in no small measure accounts for the vastly improved quality of empirical research in this field, in the face of data problems as severe as any encountered in economics proper. Kuznets was more interested in theories that proposed to describe and generalize about some aspects of the observable behavior of the economy than in those that sought the simplest set of a priori assumptions, and the weakest specification of functional relations, that could produce a particular generalization. Among the theories that he found most fruitful, but not necessarily correct, were Malthus's statements on the relation between population and economic growth, Joseph Schumpeter's theory of the business cycle, Walter Hoffmann's theory of the sequencing of industrialization, Alvin Hansen's theory of the effect of population growth on savings rates, theories about the behavior of savings over the life cycle, theories of human capital formation, theories about the factors affecting the size distribution of income, and neoclassical models of economic growth (particularly as developed by Robert Solow, Edward Denison, Zvi Griliches, and Dale Jorgenson since they implied accounting identities that, when flexibly approached, were useful in arraying data bearing on the growth process).

Kuznets appreciated the advantages of formalizing such generalizations and of demonstrating how they could be deduced from a limited set of a priori assumptions. Such work had shown that downward-sloping demand curves, perhaps the single most important analytic and empirical tool of economics, did not require the dubious, convoluted assumptions about consumer psychology of earlier theorists but could be generated from a few simple assumptions about preference orderings. The mathematical development of the theory of consumer demand also called attention to the important distinction between income and substitution effects and had a large impact on the development of statistical procedures for the estimation of demand functions.

Yet, without in any way belittling these achievements, Kuznets feared that such formalization of theory was becoming increasingly sterile, partly as the result of an overinvestment in it. Too many papers merely explored the consequences of changing one or another assumption in a given hypothetico-deductive model. Though they pointed up the sensitivity of such models to their assumptions, they rarely served as guides to study of the real economic world. Nevertheless, these intellectual exercises acquired a vogue, and those engaged in this work developed a set of standards for judging quality that had little to do with the ultimate bearing of the models on empirical research. To avoid sterility, hypothetico-deductive modeling had to be intimately connected with, and regularly infused by, findings from empirical, experimental, and clinical research, as they normally were in the natural sciences.

6 :: Further Aspects of the Legacy of Simon Kuznets

Frequent encounters with former students were a regular occurrence in Kuznets's later years. Always the teacher, he began his customary greeting with an inquiry after an individual's family, followed closely by an inquisitive, "What have you been working on lately?" Even as they became established family members and pioneers in economic history, econometrics, and cliometrics themselves, some former students never felt comfortable addressing their teacher as anything other than "Professor."

With others, Kuznets had a more jocular relationship, as with the widely heralded labor economist and demographer Richard Easterlin, of the University of Southern California. When the announcement was made that Kuznets had won the 1971 Nobel Prize in economics, Easterlin admonished his former teacher to not let the award go to his head but conceded that Kuznets "probably didn't have to worry about 'publish or perish' any longer." Then seventy years old, Kuznets considered this for a moment and then mused: "In a way—I do." He would heed his own advice, publishing over forty additional articles before his death in 1985.

In 1981, a weekend-long celebration of Kuznets's eightieth birthday was held at Harvard University. Over 150 guests, including Arthur F. Burns, John Kenneth Galbraith, Paul Samuelson, Henry Rosovsky, and Martin Feldstein, constituted a veritable who's who of economics. Easterlin, Nathan Rosenberg (Stanford), and Dwight Perkins (Harvard) presented papers considering modern economic growth.

In addition to the scheduled speakers, friends and associates spontaneously leaped to their feet to toast their friend and mentor and share anecdotes.

Kuznets passed away on a Monday in early July 1985. The *New York Times* ran his obituary the following Thursday, July 11, with the headline: "Simon Kuznets Is Dead at 84; Nobel Laureate in Economics." The obituary quoted Paul A. Samuelson, the recipient of the 1970 Nobel Prize in economics: "Simon Kuznets was a giant in twentieth century economics. He was the founder of national income measurement, and he created quantitative economic history." Indeed, it is these two particular areas of achievement that have become synonymous with his life's work.

Kuznets's legacy includes not only his many books and articles but also the students he trained, many of whom became influential economists in their own right. There is also an institutional legacy. In 1978, when Martin Feldstein became the new CEO of the NBER, he suggested to some of Kuznets's students that they establish a new program at the bureau that would continue Kuznets's work on long-term factors promoting economic growth. That program was established under the title "The Development of the American Economy," or DAE.

There were three initial projects of the DAE: "The Economics of Mortality in North America, 1650–1910" aimed to collect and analyze newly available data from archival sources to illuminate changing North American mortality rates for this three-hundred-year period. "The Economic and Demographic Significance of Secular Changes in Human Stature" aimed to trace improvements in nutrition in the United States as reflected in height data from the period 1750–1910. "The Changing Role of Women in the Labor Force" sought to examine the role of women in the labor force from the beginning of the nineteenth century, drawing from all available data, especially federal and state censuses. At the time, these research projects were among the most ambitious ever proposed in the field.

Over the next ten years, a number of additional projects were added to the DAE, all of which focused on long-term factors contributing to economic growth in the United States. The DAE marked a departure from the NBER's approach of looking at growth on a macroeconomic level (such as national income accounts). With the creation of over fifty new data sets in their first ten years, DAE researchers were able to examine the economy on a microeconomic level. These data sets followed individuals, families, and firms.

DAE research was substantial and produced several significant achievements in the program's first decade. The "Labor and Population" project used census data to revise the existing estimates of the distribution of the labor force between farm and nonfarm industries. The data collected showed that the existing estimates had been overstated for a time and then understated. Thomas Weiss published several working papers summarizing his findings and concluding that, between 1820 and 1860, the farm labor force grew more rapidly than had been thought previously but that farm productivity and per capita actually grew more slowly (see Weiss 1986, 1987, 1989). Later research revealed that exports were not as important a stimulus to economic growth in the American South as had previously been thought. The project "Female Labor Force and Gender Distinctions in the Labor Process," led by Claudia Goldin, found that the ratio of female-to-male earnings rose between 1815 and 1930 and then stabilized until 1980. The expansion of occupations held by married women after World War II was linked to expansions in education and clerical work in the 1920s and 1930s. These and other findings by Goldin were collected in *Understanding the Gender Gap* (1990), which illustrated women's role in the modern workforce as the culmination of trends that began two centuries earlier rather than as abrupt social shifts.

The project "Secular Trends in Nutrition, Labor Welfare, and Labor Productivity," which brought together several researchers in the construction of anthropometric measures of standards of living, was facilitated by innovative new statistical procedures (see Trussell and Wachter 1984). The nutrition branch of the project discovered that the standard of living with regard to nutrition in the colonial period was high, even by modern standards. Findings showed that adult slaves were well nourished as adults, less so as children. The average heights of the British during the eighteenth and nineteenth centuries generally exceeded those of populations in other countries (except for the United States).

One of the DAE's major accomplishments was bringing a Kuznetsian tradition of long-term, data-driven quantitative research into the computer age. Collection and calculation that previously took months could potentially be completed in a matter of hours. To realize that potential, the DAE had to develop new procedures for the retrieval, management, and analysis of data as well as ferret out the data sets that would be examined.

When the DAE project "The Economics of Mortality in North America" began in 1976, it initially examined the potential usefulness of genealogies covering 1 million individuals in about 200,000 families, linked intergenerationally for up to ten generations. The initial effort of measurement, however, involved the collection of a sample of 13,000 white men mustered into the Union army between 1861 and 1865. Their records contained data on height and twelve other variables, yielding altogether about fifty characters of information per individuals. This information was copied by hand onto sheets that were then entered into computers. At around ten minutes per individual, it took about two thousand person-hours to complete the project.

By 1981, investigators collecting a new sample of 40,000 Union army soldiers were using portable terminals with rewritable "bubble memory" that had a capacity of 100,000 characters, about what an experienced typist would produce in a day. With the built-in modems, investigators were able to transfer the contents of the memory to the mainframe computers overnight. Even with the required cleaning of the data, the new technology had reduced the cost of data collection by about 80 percent.

This reduction in costs had implications that went beyond the amount of funding necessary to collect the original body of data: advances in technology made possible projects that had previously been prohibitively expensive. The comprehensive project that grew from this earlier project, "The Aging of Union Army Men: A Longitudinal Study, 1830–1940," set out to create a public-use data set from a sample of men mustered into the Union army. With these data, investigators intended to examine the effect of nutritional and socioeconomic status at early ages on work levels, morbidity, and mortality rates at later ages. The complete life-cycle information for a single recruit contained fifteen thousand variables—an unthinkable amount of data for the portable computers of the mid-1980s.[1] This project merged into a large study, "Early Indicators of Later Work Levels, Disease, and Death," first funded by the National Institute of Aging in 1991 and recently renewed through 2015. This far-reaching study, which has made many surprising discoveries over the past twenty years, has produced, to date, over 250 books, dissertations, articles, and working papers.

Research under the auspices of the DAE continues under the direction of Claudia Goldin. The membership of the DAE has increased from only seven at the beginning to over sixty today. Recent research has examined topics as broad as the contribution of the potato to population and urbanization, issues of land policy, and fluctuations in overseas travel by Americans between 1820 and 2000. DAE researchers continue to examine some of the classic topics of economic history, including railroads and industrialization, the banking situation during the Great Depression, and even the economic impact of the U.S. Constitution (Nunn and Quian 2009; Grubb 2011; Dupont, Gandhi, and Weiss 2009; Atack, Haines, and Margo 2008; Richardson and Van Horn 2008).

The Conference on Research in Income and Wealth

The NBER's Conference on Research in Income and Wealth (CRIW) was founded in 1935, "a brainchild of Simon Kuznets," in the words of Milton Friedman. Born as a collaboration between the NBER and the economics departments of six universities (Columbia and Harvard Universities and the Universities of Chicago, Minnesota, Pennsylvania, and Wisconsin), the CRIW aimed to serve as a liaison between the NBER, academics, businesses, and government to facilitate research. Income and wealth were agreed to be subjects of particular relevance that the bureau excelled at examining (Carson 1990).

In 1937, the CRIW published the first volume of the series *Studies*

---

1. With the introduction of laptops, graduate students could independently undertake projects that would have required extensive funding just a few years earlier. Furthermore, as computers allowed more variables to be incorporated in models, the distance between theorists and empiricists was narrowing.

in Income and Wealth, which outlined the research plan for the conference. In a preface that set the tone for the scope of the work that was to be undertaken, Wesley Mitchell wrote: "Those who have not wrestled long with the highly technical problems that crop up in such work can scarcely appreciate their intricacy, or how considerable are the differences in results that are produced by the use of slightly different definitions" (Mitchell 1937, viii).

Fittingly, one of the early accomplishments of the conference was the standardization of terminology. A committee, headed by Kuznets, was formed "to promote a greater uniformity of usage" (quoted in Carson 1990, 5). Among the accomplishments of this committee was the clarification of the distinction between *national income produced* and *national income paid out*, two terms that differentiate between, respectively, figures that include saving by businesses and figures that do not. This distinction underlaid questions among economists as to what should and should not be included in calculations of national income.

Another important area of research that fell within the purview of the CRIW was the foundational research for the preparation of distributions of income by the different deciles of population size. The lack of such figures was considered to be a chief deficit in income research. A committee consisting of Milton Friedman, Dorothy Brady, Clark Warburton, and C. Lowell Harris was charged with investigating this issue; it produced the fifth in the series of CRIW publications, *Income Size Distributions in the United States* (CRIW 1943). This volume, with an introductory chapter by Kuznets, provided a summary of the most important studies of U.S. income distribution to date and recommended future research directions (see Carson 1990).

The conference has continued to hold annual meetings and has produced seventy books examining issues in economic measurement and measurements of output and productivity. Unlike other programs at the bureau, the CRIW has its own federal funding to conduct its research on measurement. In a 2005 article in the *NBER Reporter*, Charles R. Hulton commemorated the fiftieth anniversary of the conference by highlighting some of the most significant contributions of the research, which addressed deficits in measurement techniques.

The CRIW was among the first to call for revision of the methods of measurements to include the impact of the information technology revolution, which had previously been elusive—Robert Solow observed, "You can see the computer revolution everywhere but in the productivity statistics" (1987, 36), a concern that was later echoed by Alan Greenspan. Later research by the Boskin Commission, a group chosen to examine the consumer price index, determined that the reported rise in prices was one-third too high because of the failure to take account of the impact of technological change on prices.

The Committee on Economic Growth

Another significant research program that was organized by Kuznets was the Committee on Economic Growth at the Social Science Research Council (SSRC). This program was born from President John F. Kennedy's concern over the amount of gold that the United States was sending overseas to countries that were experiencing tremendous growth over the 1950s, a practice that wreaked havoc with the exchange rate. In an effort to come to grips with this, the Kennedy administration commissioned two studies: one on growth accounts, to be headed by Edward Denison, and a set of long-term historical studies that would examine growth in an international sample of rich nations, to be headed by Simon Kuznets.

When Kuznets approached Wesley Mitchell about the possibility of examining the economic development of nations around the world at the NBER, he encountered a less-than-enthusiastic response. This led to Kuznets's affiliation with the SSRC, begun in 1949, when he headed up a research program, funded by the Rockefeller Foundation, to examine the process of international economic growth. To facilitate the enterprise, the SSRC established the Committee on Economic Growth, which consisted of a distinguished set of economists who set out to explore "possible directions of empirical research on long-term changes in magnitude and structure of larger social units, such as nations, and regions of the United States" (*Items* [SSRC] 3, no. 1 [1949]: 7). In 1951, the decision was made to host a conference, arranged jointly with the Committee on Social Implications of Atomic

Energy and Technological Change, to discuss quantifiable measurement of technological change and "to consider the problems relating to the industrialization of three countries: India, Japan, and Brazil" (*Items* 5, no. 1 [1951]: 8). The conference was held in April 1952 to "weigh the possibilities of adding to knowledge through the comparative study of economic growth, 'possibilities' being judged with respect to the establishment of verifiable explanations of why growth has or has not taken place, and only incidentally with respect to current national or international policy issues" (*Items* 6, no. 2 [1952]: 22).

Three major works came out of this project: *French Economic Growth* (Carre, Dubois, and Malinvaud 1975); *British Economic Growth* (Matthews, Feinstein, and Odling-Smee 1982); and *Japanese Economic Growth* (Okawa and Rosovsky 1973). Many of the smaller projects, including an investigation of U.S. growth trends that was headed by Moses Abramovitz, were not completed, although they did produce a few papers. Although the committee failed to realize its initial lofty aims, it is important to realize that these three volumes in particular provided background on economic growth that had been neglected by the literature—chapters on the sweeping cultural changes that sustained the rapid advances in material growth that these countries experienced.

Kuznets's Lasting Contributions to Economics

Kuznets's work on national income accounting and the creation of measures of GDP are among his most lasting and influential contributions.[2] GDP continues to be the benchmark measure of the health of a nation's economy, relied on by policymakers at the national level. In 1999, Commerce secretary William Daley, joined by Federal Reserve chief Alan Greenspan and Martin Baily, chairman of the Council of Economic Advisers, paid tribute to this statistic and the economists who helped develop it at an awards ceremony. "Without the big picture the GDP gives us," Daley said, "[Greenspan and Baily] would not have the information they need to figure out what's going on in our

2. GDP is a slight variant of GNP.

economy and take appropriate action" (Berry 1999, E3). Organizations such as the International Monetary Fund and the World Bank rely on GDP measures to make funding decisions.

Now that the existence of measures of national income are taken for granted, GDP is more likely to be maligned for its deficits than celebrated for closing a gaping void in the policymaking process. It therefore bears repeating that the trailblazing Kuznets never oversold the application of GDP. Testifying to Congress in 1937, he emphasized: "The welfare of a nation can scarcely be inferred from a measurement of national income" (Kuznets 1934, 7). The prescriptions for these problems proposed in recent years, such as the human development index (HDI), owe a debt to Kuznets. The HDI has been computed by the UN Development Programme annually since 1990. In an effort to quantify the "process of enlarging people's choices" ("Human Development Initiative Programme," n.d.), the HDI is the average of combined measures of education, health, and the standard of living, which is based on a measure of GDP.

Kuznets is responsible for establishing a tradition of rigorous, disciplined research in economics in its early years as a quantitative science even with the data that was available to him, a shockingly small amount when compared to the vast stores of data that are now only as far away as the nearest laptop. He worked with and influenced some of the greatest economic minds of his generation, both colleagues and students. It may be that his greatest legacy is that of a teacher who nurtured the curiosity and tradition of rigorous research that took economics from the relatively small, insular discipline that it had been to the hugely influential science that it has become. His influence is felt in the best of policy-oriented research being conducted today.

7 : : The Quarter Century since the Death of Simon Kuznets

More than a quarter century has passed since the death of Simon Kuznets. The population of the United States today is more than a third larger than it was in 1985. And the total U.S. economy has doubled. Major new technological innovations such as the Internet, e-mail, and laptop computers have transformed communication, education, and research. Although some of the details of the new technology might have surprised Kuznets, the general thrust would not.

Kuznets expected technological innovation to accelerate, partly because of the larger number of people available to tackle the challenges, and partly because of the inherent tendency of the economy to reach and supersede successive ceilings. He recognized that this scenario required a progrowth culture and that such a culture was not inevitable. Not all societies are willing to trade present leisure for higher output in the future. He presumed that for, the foreseeable future, the progrowth culture would dominate a culture of leisure in the highly developed nations.

However, optimism was in the air during the post–World War II years when recessions were usually short and mild and recoveries were long and vigorous. The average recession following World War II lasted only eleven months, and the average recovery lasted about five years. Kuznets died during an exceptionally vigorous recovery that lasted nearly eight years.

The next several business cycles also had short, mild recessions and vigorous recoveries. It was not until the last year of the last Bush administration and the first two years of the Obama administration that the country lapsed into a severe recession again. The current use of Keynesian antirecession policies failed to reinvigorate the economy, and the government share of GDP grew from 20 to 24 percent without significantly reducing unemployment. Although the recession finally came to an end at the start of 2012, the recovery has been anemic, with official unemployment rates hovering around 8 percent. Including voluntary withdrawals by discouraged workers, total unemployment was in the neighborhood of 16 percent.

In most post–World War II recoveries, the rate of growth of GDP has been about 6 percent, but, under current policies, the growth rate has sputtered between 1 and 3 percent. It will probably take some time before the data needed to explain adequately the course of the economy under the Obama administration are available.

However, in March 2012, the Conference Board, a nonpartisan research institution, announced that it was likely that economic conditions would continue to improve throughout the first half of 2012 (Conference Board 2012). Moreover, that same month Larry Summers, Secretary of the Treasury under President Clinton and one of Obama's early economic advisers, concluded that reducing government intervention in the economy could seriously compromise the recovery (Summers 2012).

But is the type of governmental intervention that emphasizes the redistribution of income from the rich to the poor adequate to counteract the high unemployment rate? This policy contrasts sharply with those of such previous Democratic presidents as John F. Kennedy, Jimmy Carter, and Bill Clinton, who put their main emphasis on promoting economic growth, trusting that a rising tide would raise all boats and high income would finance redistributive programs such as Medicare.

Another significant change that the last quarter century has seen is growth in Asia. Kuznets was aware of the acceleration of growth in Asia, but with the exception of Japan, where reliable data were available going back to the late nineteenth century, there was little long-term information about the region. Even for the third quarter of the twentieth century, reliable information on levels and growth rates of population, income, and education levels for India and Korea were seen as shaky by scholars of these countries. In the case of China, many Western scholars questioned the believability of the statistical information released by the government and viewed it more as propaganda than as information.

In 1993, the World Bank published an influential monograph called *The East Asian Miracle* that focused on economic growth in Japan and seven other high-performing Asian economies: South Korea, Taiwan, Singapore, Hong Kong, Indonesia, Malaysia, and Thailand. These countries, it showed, were growing faster than any other region of the world between 1965 and 1990 (although it was noted parenthetically that China was also in the midst of an economic miracle). In its conclusion, the report singled out the essential policies for rapid economic growth, stressing macroeconomic stability, low inflation, competitive exchange rates, and high investment in education.

Beyond many technical issues about how to interpret the available information, there is a lively debate about how long China can continue growth at rates greater than ever before achieved for long periods of time. China has emerged as a major global factor in an array of product markets. Now second only to the United States in oil consumption and accounting for 40 percent of all the growth in global oil consumption in recent years, it has also become the world's largest consumer of steel, cement, and copper.

Most of China's growth in terms of per capita income (69 percent between 1978 and 2002) is due to increases in labor productivity. Within industry, there was an increase of 6.2 percent per annum in labor productivity and 5.7 percent per annum in agriculture. About 30 percent of China's growth rate is likely to continue to come from modest increases in the labor force participation rate and interindustry shifts. Much of its labor force is still in agriculture, so there is substantial potential for growth through a shift to industry and services as it moves toward the current technological frontier.

Investment in capital—especially human capital—is capable of rapid development in the next several decades. A college-educated worker is 3.1 times as productive, and a high school graduate 1.8 times as productive, as a worker with less than a ninth-grade education, underlining the potential for growth. Ownership of automobiles and other major consumer durable products has also been increasing at spectacular rates. Between 1990 and 2007, Chinese households have increased ownership of air conditioners annually by 15 percent, computers by 32 percent, and cell phones by 48 percent. In 2011, China became the world's leading producer and consumer of automobiles.

The rapidly expanding economies of China and India have led many analysts to speculate on the reemergence of these two economic giants as global political players. The National Intelligence Council recently conjectured that, by 2025, U.S. political dominance will be replaced by what it calls *multipolarity*. This multipolarity is, it predicts, "unlikely to produce a single dominant nation-state with the overwhelming power and legitimacy to act as an agent of institutional overhaul" (National Intelligence Council 2008, 81). However, we are already in a multipolar world, one that the United States helped create. Our ability to influence international affairs is already constrained by the desires of Europe, Russia, India, and China. Diplomacy under the Clinton and Bush administrations was shaped by such recognition.

Our own view of future U.S. global influence is more conditional. A lot depends on the future rate of growth of U.S. labor productivity. If that continues at the annual rate of 2–4 percent, then it is possible that the United States will remain well ahead of its competitors in economic and political influence down to 2025 and beyond. Much will depend on the willingness of the United States to invest heavily in scientific research and development and to increase the share of the population educated in the sciences. We are optimistic on both these counts. Unlike China, whose past growth has depended on its ability to adapt to the existing technology of the United States and other OECD nations, the United States is at the current production frontier. Hence, its continued growth depends on the rate at which it can develop new technologies, a process that requires a plentiful supply of engineers to design new systems of production and distribution and new science on which these new systems will depend. Industry will respond to the new technologies, as they have in the past, because they will increase labor productivity and raise profits.

Acknowledgments

The authors are grateful to the National Bureau of Economic Research, which supported a series of interviews with prominent economists conducted by the Fogels. These interviews greatly informed this book, particularly those with John Kenneth Galbraith, Robert Nathan, and Paul Samuelson.

We thank also the Kuznets Archive at Harvard University for its assistance with research. It would not have been possible to complete the book without helpful comments and assistance from Joseph Burton, Louis P. Cain, Paul A. David, Richard Easterlin, Claudia Goldin, Dale Jorgenson, Dwight Perkins, and Henry Rosovsky. Our thanks are also due to Paul Kuznets and Judy Stein. David Pervin at the University of Chicago Press has been a keen editor, and his input has improved the final product greatly.

References

Abramovitz, M. 1952. "Economics of Growth." In *A Survey of Contemporary Economics, Volume 2*, ed. B. F. Haley, 132–78. Homewood, IL: Richard D. Irwin.

———. 1971. "Nobel Prize for Economics: Kuznets and Economic Growth." *Science*, October 29, 481–83.

———. 1985. "Simon Kuznets: An Appreciation." Photocopy, Department of Economics, Stanford University.

———. 1990. "The Catch-Up Factor in Postwar Economic Growth." *Economic Inquiry* 28:1–18.

Adams, T. S. 1916. Review of *Income: An Examination of the Returns for Services Rendered and from Property Owned in the United States*, by S. Nearing. *American Economic Review* 6, no. 1:182–87.

Alchon, G. 1985. *The Invisible Hand of Planning: Capitalism, Social Science, and the State in the 1920*. Princeton, NJ: Princeton University Press.

Aldrich, N. 1892. "Retail Prices and Wages Report by Mr. Aldrich from Committee on Finance." S. Rep. 986. 52nd Cong., 1st sess., July 19.

———. 1893. "Wholesale Prices, Wages, and Transportation." Report from the Committee on Finance. S. Rep. 1394, 52nd Cong., 2nd sess., March 3.

"American President: Herbert Hoover (1874–1964)." n.d. Available at http://millercenter.org/president/hoover.

Anand, S., and S. M. R. Kanbur. 1984. "Inequality and Development: A Reconsideration." In *Towards Income Distribution Policies: From Income Distribution Research to Income Distribution Policy in LDCs* (Book Series no. 3), ed. H. P. Nissen, 131–67. Tilburg: EADI.

———. 1987. "International Poverty Projections." Paper presented at UNU/WIDER Conference on Poverty, Undernutrition, and Living Standards, Helsinki, Finland, July 27–31.

———. 1993. "The Kuznets Process and the Inequality-Development Relationship." *Journal of Development Economics* 40:25–52.

Atack, J., M. R. Haines, and R. A. Margo. 2008. "Railroads and the Rise of the Factory: Evidence for the United States, 1850–70." Working Paper no. w14410. Cambridge, MA: NBER.

Barber, W. J. 1985. *From New Order to New Deal*. New York: Cambridge University Press.

———. 1996. *Designs within Disorder: Franklin D. Roosevelt, the Economists, and the Shaping of American Economic Policy, 1933–1945*. Cambridge: Cambridge University Press.

Bascom, J. 1859. *Political Economy: Designed as a Text-Book for Colleges*. Andover, MA: W. F. Draper.

Becker, G. 1960. "An Economic Analysis of Fertility." In *Demographic and Economic Change in Developed Countries: Conference of the Universities–National Bureau Committee for Economic Research: A Report of the National Bureau of Economic Research*, 209–40. Princeton, NJ: Princeton University Press.

———. 1981. *A Treatise on the Family*. Cambridge, MA: Harvard University Press.

Becker, G., and H. G. Lewis. 1973. "On the Interaction between Quantity and Quality of Children." *Journal of Political Economy* 81:S279–S288.

Ben-Porath, Y. 1986. "Simon Kuznets in Person and Writing." Discussion Paper no. 86.08. Jerusalem: Maurice Falk Institute for Economic Research in Israel.

Benson, L. 1955. *Merchants, Farmers and Railroads: Railroad Regulation and New York Politics, 1850–1887*. Cambridge, MA: Harvard University Press.

Bergson, A. 1986. "Simon Kuznets: 30 April 1901–8 July 1985." *American Philosophical Yearbook*, 134–38.

Bergson, A., H. Leibenstein, H. Rosovsky, and Z. Griliches. 1987. "Faculty of Arts and Sciences—Memorial Minute: Simon Kuznets." Minute place on the record at a meeting of the Harvard University faculty, December 16, 1986. *Harvard Gazette*, March 20.

Berndt, E. R., and J. E. Triplett. 1992. *Fifty Years of Economic Measurement: The Jubilee of the Conference on Research in Income and Wealth*. Chicago: University of Chicago Press.

Bernstein, M. 2001. *A Perilous Progress: Economists and Political Purpose in Twentieth-Century America*. Princeton, NJ: Princeton University Press.

Berry, J. M. 1999. "3 Cheers for 3 Letters: G-D-P; for Commerce, It's the Stat of the Century." *Washington Post*, December 8, E3.

Blaug, M. 1980. *The Methodology of Economics*. Cambridge: Cambridge University Press.

Böhm-Bawerk, E. von. 1890. *Capital and Interest: A Critical History of Economical Theory*. London: Macmillan.

Boltho, A. 1975. "Review: *Japanese Economic Growth*." *Econometrica* 42:454–56.

Bowman, J. S. 1995. *The Cambridge Dictionary of American Biography*. New York: Cambridge University Press.

Bowman, M. J. 1980. "On Theodore W. Schultz's Contributions to Economics." *Scandinavian Journal of Economics* 82, no. 1: 80–107.

Bratt, E. C. 1953. "A Reconsideration of the Postwar Forecasts." *Journal of Business of the University of Chicago* 26:71–83.

Brigante, J. E. 1950. "The Feasibility Dispute: Determination of War Production Objectives for 1942 and 1943." Committee on Public Administration Cases. Washington, DC: U.S. Government Printing Office.

Brown, E. C. 1956. "Fiscal Policy in the Thirties: A Reappraisal." *American Economic Review* 46:857–79.

Brownlee, E. 1990. "Economists and the Formation of the Modern Tax System in the

United States: The World War I Crisis." In *The State and Economic Knowledge: The American and British Experiences*, ed. M. O. Furner and B. E. Supple, 401–34. Cambridge: Cambridge University Press.

Burns, A. F. 1952. "Introductory Sketch." In *Wesley Clair Mitchell: The Economic Scientist*, ed. A. F. Burns, 1–54. New York: NBER.

Burns, J. M. 1956. *Roosevelt: The Lion and the Fox*. San Diego: Harcourt, Brace & World.

Carre, J. J., P. Dubois, and E. Malinvaud. 1975. *French Economic Growth*. London: Oxford University Press.

Carson, C. S. 1990. "The Conference on Research in Income and Wealth: The Early Years." In *Fifty Years of Economic Measurement*, ed. E. R. Berndt and J. E. Triplett, 3–8. Chicago: University of Chicago Press.

Chow, G. 2006. "Are Chinese Official Statistics Reliable?" *CESifo Economic Studies* 52:396–414.

Clark, J. M. 1931. "Wesley C. Mitchell's Contribution to the Theory of Business Cycles." In *Methods in Social Science: A Casebook*, ed. S. A. Rice, 193–206. Chicago: University of Chicago Press.

Colm, G. 1962. "Capital in the American Economy: Its Formation and Financing." *Journal of the American Statistical Association* 57:693–96.

Committee on Business Cycles and Unemployment of the President's Conference on Unemployment. 1923. *Business Cycles and Unemployment*. New York: NBER.

Committee on Recent Economic Changes of the President's Conference on Unemployment. 1929. *Recent Economic Changes in the United States*. 2 vols. New York: McGraw-Hill, for NBER. Available online at http://www.nber.org/chapters/c4950.pdf.

Conference Board. 2012. "Global Business Cycle Indicators." March 22. Available at http://www.conference-board.org/data/bciarchive.cfm?cid=1&pid=4436.

Conference on Research in Income and Wealth (CRIW). 1943. *Income Size Distributions in the United States*. New York: NBER.

Cook, P. B. 1982. *Academicians in Government from Roosevelt to Roosevelt*. New York: Garland.

Crafts, N. F. R. 1975. "Review: *Japanese Economic Growth*." *Economic History Review* 28:165–66.

Crafts, N. F. R., and G. Toniolo. 1996. *Economic Growth in Europe since 1945*. Cambridge: Cambridge University Press.

Creedy, J. 1992. *Demand and Exchange in Economic Analysis: A History from Cournot to Marshall*. Aldershot: Edward Elgar.

Cuff, R. D. 1989. "Creating Control Systems: Edwin F. Gay and the Central Bureau of Planning and Statistics, 1917–1919." *Business History Review* 63, no. 3:588–613.

Curti, M., and V. Carstensen. 1949. *The University of Wisconsin: A History, 1848–1925*. 2 vols. Madison: University of Wisconsin Press.

David, P. A. 1967. "The Growth of Real Product in the United States before 1840." *Journal of Economic History* 27:151–57.

Davis, L. E., and R. A. Huttenback. 1986. *Mammon and the Pursuit of Empire: The Political Economy of British Imperialism, 1860–1912*. Cambridge: Cambridge University Press.

Deane, P. 1967. "Book Reviews: *Modern Economic Growth: Rate, Structure and Spread*." *Economic Journal* 77 (December): 882–83.

Debreu, G. 1984. "Economic Theory in the Mathematical Mode." *American Economic Review* 74, no. 3:267–78.

Denison, E. F. 1967. "Sources of Postwar Growth in Nine Western Countries." *American Economic Review* 57:325–32.

de Rouvray, C. 2004. "'Old' Economic History in the United States: 1939–1954." *Journal of the History of Economic Thought* 26, no. 2:221–39.

Dorfman, J. 1946. *The Economic Mind in American Civilization*. Vol. 2, *1606–1865*. New York: Viking.

———. 1959a. *The Economic Mind in American Civilization*. Vol. 3, *1865–1918*. New York: Viking.

———. 1959b. *The Economic Mind in American Civilization*. Vol. 4, *1918–1933*. New York: Viking.

Duncan, J. W., and W. C. Shelton. 1978. *Revolution in United States Government Statistics, 1926–1976*. Washington, DC: U.S. Department of Commerce.

Dupont, B., A. Gandhi, and T. Weiss. 2009. "Fluctuations in Overseas Travel by Americans, 1820–2000." Working Paper no. w14847. Cambridge, MA: NBER.

Easterlin, R. A. 1989. Foreword to *Economic Development, the Family, and Income Distribution: Selected Essays*, by S. Kuznets, 1–6. Cambridge: Cambridge University Press.

Edelstein, M. 2001. "The Size of the US Armed Forces during World War II: Feasibility and War Planning." *Research in Economic History* 20:47–97.

Engerman, S. L., and R. E. Gallman. 1983. "U.S. Economic Growth." *Research in Economic History* 8:1–46.

Fabricant, S. 1984. "Toward a Firmer Basis of Economic Policy: The Founding of the National Bureau of Economic Research." http://www.nber.org/nberhistory/sfabricantrev .pdf (accessed September 6, 2011).

Fei, J. C. H., G. Ranis, and S. W. Y. Kuo. 1978. "Growth and the Family Distribution of Income by Factor Components." *Quarterly Journal of Economics* 92:17–53.

Fields, G. S. 1980. *Poverty, Inequality and Development*. Cambridge: Cambridge University Press.

Fisher, I. 1919. "Economists in Public Service: Annual Address of the President." *American Economic Review* 9, no. 1:5.

Floud, R., R. W. Fogel, B. Harris, and S. C. Hong. 2011. *The Changing Body: Health, Nutrition, and Human Development in the Western World since 1700*. New York: Cambridge University Press.

Fogel, R. W. 1964. *Railroads and American Economic Growth: Essays in Econometric History*. Baltimore: Johns Hopkins University Press.

———. 1970. "Historiography and Retrospective Econometrics." *History and Theory* 9:245–64.

———. 1992. "Problems in Modeling Complex Dynamic Interactions: The Political Realignment of the 1850s." *Economics and Politics* 4:215–54.

———. 1999. "Catching Up with the Economy (Presidential Lecture)." *American Economic Review* 89:1–21.

———. 2000. *The Fourth Great Awakening and the Future of Egalitarianism*. Chicago: University of Chicago Press.

———. 2003. "Forecasting the Demand for Health Care in OECD Nations and China." *Contemporary Economic Policy* 21:1–10.

———. 2004. *The Escape from Hunger and Premature Death, 1700–2100: Europe, America, and the Third World*. New York: Cambridge University Press.

———. 2005. "Reconsidering Expectations of Economic Growth after World War II from the Perspective of 2004." Working Paper no. 11125. Cambridge, MA: NBER.

———. 2007. "Capitalism and Democracy in 2040." *Daedalus* 136, no. 3 (Summer): 87–95.

———. 2009a. "Economic and Social Structure for an Ageing Population." In *Sociology of Ageing: A Reader*, ed. A. K. Sahoo, G. J. Andrews, and S. I. Rajan, 121–42. New Delhi: Rawat.

———. 2009b. "The Impact of the Asian Miracle on the Theory of Economic Growth." Working Paper no. 14967. Cambridge, MA: NBER.

Fogel, R. W., and S. L. Engerman. 1969. "A Model for the Explanation of Industrial Expansion during the Nineteenth Century: With an Application to the American Iron Industry." *Journal of Political Economy* 77:306–28.

———. 1992a. *Without Consent or Contract: Markets and Production, Technical Papers, Volume 1*. New York: Norton.

———. 1992b. *Without Consent or Contract: Conditions of Slave Life and The Transition to Freedom, Technical Papers, Volume 2*. New York: Norton.

Fogel, R. W., R. A. Galantine, and R. L. Manning. 1992. *Without Consent or Contract: Evidence and Methods*. New York: Norton.

Furner, M. O. 1990. "Knowing Capitalism: Public Investigation and the Labor Question in the Long Progressive Era." In *The State and Economic Knowledge: The American and British Experiences*, ed. M. O. Furner and B. E. Supple, 241–86. Washington, DC: Woodrow Wilson International Center for Scholars; Cambridge: Cambridge University Press.

Gay, E. F., and W. C. Mitchell. 1929. *Annual Report of the Directors of Research*. New York: NBER.

———. 1933. *Message of the President: Report of the Directors of Research for the Year 1932*. New York: NBER.

Goldin, C. 1990. *Understanding the Gender Gap: An Economic History of American Women*. Cambridge: Cambridge University Press.

Grubb, F. 2011. "U.S. Land Policy: Founding Choices and Outcomes, 1781–1802." In *Founding Choices: American Economic Policy in the 1790s*, ed. D. Irwin and R. Sylla, 259–89. Chicago: University of Chicago Press, for NBER.

Guglielmo, M. 2008. "The Contribution of Economists to Military Intelligence during World War II." *Journal of Economic History* 68:109–50.

Hansen, A. 1939. "Economic Progress and Declining Population Growth." *American Economic Review* 29:1–15.

Hawley, E. W. 1974. "Herbert Hoover, the Commerce Secretariat, and the Vision of an 'Associative State,' 1921–1928." *Journal of American History* 61:116–40.

———. 1990. "Economic Inquiry and the State in New Era America: Antistatist Corporatism and Positive Statism in Uneasy Coexistence." In *The State and Economic Knowledge*, ed. M. O. Furner and B. E. Supple, eds., 287–324. Cambridge: Cambridge University Press.

Heaton, H. 1952. *A Scholar in Action: Edwin F. Gay*. Cambridge, MA: Harvard University Press.

———. 1968. *A Scholar in Action: Edwin F. Gay*. New York: Greenwood.

Henderson, J. P. 1993. "Political Economy and the Service of the State: The University of Wisconsin." In *Economics and Higher Learning in the Nineteenth Century*, ed. W. J. Barber, 318–39. New Brunswick, NJ: Transaction.

Hicks, G. 1989. "The Four Little Dragons: An Enthusiast's Reading Guide." *Asian-Pacific Economic Literature* 3:35–49.

Hollander, J. H. 1922. "The Economist's Spiral." *American Economic Review* 12, no. 1:9.

Hughes, J. R. T. 1991. *The Governmental Habit Redux: Economic Controls from Colonial Times to the Present*. Princeton, NJ: Princeton University Press.

Hughes, J., and L. P. Cain. 2002. *American Economic History*. 6th ed. Boston: Addison-Wesley.

———. 2007. *American Economic History*. 7th ed. New York: Prentice-Hall.

Hulten, C. R. 2005. "The Conference on Research in Income and Wealth." *NBER Reporter*, Summer 2005, 1–4.

"Human Development Initiative Programme." n.d. Available at http://www.unescap.org/drpad/vc/conference/bg_mm_15_fao.htm.

"Inaugural Address of Herbert Hoover." 1929. Washington, DC, March 4. Available at http://avalon.law.yale.edu/20th_century/hoover.asp.

Jevons, W. S. 1970. *The Theory of Political Economy*. Edited by R. D. C. Black. Harmondsworth: Penguin.

Jorgenson, D. W. 1991. "Productivity and Economic Growth." In *Fifty Years of Economic Measurement: The Jubilee of the Conference on Research in Income and Wealth*, ed. E. R. Berndt and J. E. Tripplett, 19–118. Chicago: University of Chicago Press.

Joynt, C., and N. Rescher. 1961. "The Problem of Uniqueness in History." *History and Theory* 1:150–62.

Kato, T. 2004. "Can the East Asian Miracle Persist?" Remarks by Takatoshi Kato, deputy managing director, International Monetary Fund, at Princeton University. December 2. http://www.imf.org/external/np/speeches/2004/120204.htm (accessed February 2, 2009).

Keene, A. T. 2000. "Taussig, Frank William." In *American National Biography Online*. http://www.anb.org/articles/14/14-00620.html (accessed May 21, 2009).

Kennedy, D. M. 1999. *Freedom from Fear: The American People in Depression and War, 1929–1945*. New York: Oxford University Press.

Kestenbaum, D., and J. Goldstein. 2012. "The Secret Document That Transformed China." NPR.org, January 12. http://www.npr.org/blogs/money/2012/01/20/145360447/the-secret-document-that-transformed-china (accessed February 21, 2012).

Keynes, J. M. 1936. *The General Theory of Employment, Interest and Money*. New York: Harcourt, Brace.

King, W. I. 1915. *The Wealth and Income of the People of the United States*. New York: Macmillan.

———. 1923. *Employment Hours and Earnings in Prosperity and Depression, United States, 1920–1922*. New York: NBER.

Knauth, O. W. 1922. *Distribution of Income by States in 1919*. New York: Harcourt, Brace.

Kravis, I. B. 1970. "Trade as a Handmaiden of Growth: Similarities between the Nineteenth and Twentieth Centuries." *Economic Journal* 80:850–72.

Krishnan, R. R. 1982. "The South Korean 'Miracle': Sell-Out to Japan, US." *Social Scientist* 10:25–37.

Krugman, P. 1994. "The Myth of Asia's Miracle." *Foreign Affairs* 73:62–79. http://full access.foreignaffairs.org/19941101faessay5151/paul-krugman/the-myth-of-asia-s -miracle.html (accessed November 10, 2008).

———. 1998. "What Happened to Asia?" Conference paper. http://web.mit.edu/ krugman/www/DISINTER.html (accessed November 17, 2008).

Krugman, P., and R. Wells. 2005. *Macroeconomics*. New York: Worth.

Kuisel, R. F. 1975. "Review: *Abrégé de la croissance française*." *French Review* 48:943–44.

Kuznets, S. 1934. "National Income, 1929–1932." S. Doc. 124, 73rd Cong., 2d sess.

———. 1952a. "Long-Term Changes in the National Income of the United States of America since 1870." In *Income and Wealth of the United States: Trends and Structure* (International Association for Research in Income and Wealth), 29–241. Cambridge: Bowes & Bowes.

———. 1952b. "National Income Estimates for the United States prior to 1870." *Journal of Economic History* 12:115–30.

———. 1955. "Economic Growth and Income Inequality." *American Economic Review: Papers and Proceedings* 45:1–28. Presidential address.

———. 1956. "Quantitative Aspects of the Economic Growth of Nations: 1, Levels and Variability of Rates of Growth." *Economic Development and Cultural Change*, vol. 5, no. 1 (October).

———. 1957. "Quantitative Aspects of the Economic Growth of Nations: 2, Industrial Distribution of National Product and Labor Force." *Economic Development and Cultural Change*, vol. 5, no. 4, suppl. (July).

———. 1960. "Quantitative Aspects of the Economic Growth of Nations: 5, Capital Formation Proportions: International Comparisons for Recent Years." *Economic Development and Cultural Change*, vol. 8, no. 4, pt. 2 (July).

———. 1961a. *Capital in the American Economy: Its Formation and Financing*. Princeton, NJ: Princeton University Press.

———. 1961b. "Quantitative Aspects of the Economic Growth of Nations: 6, Long-Term Trends in Capital Formation Proportions." *Economic Development and Cultural Change*, vol. 9, no. 4, pt. 2 (July).

———. 1962. "Quantitative Aspects of the Economic Growth of Nations: 7, The Share and Structures of Consumption." *Economic Development and Cultural Change*, vol. 10, no. 2, pt. 2 (January).

———. 1963. "Quantitative Aspects of the Economic Growth of Nations: 8, Distribution of Income by Size." *Economic Development and Cultural Change*, vol. 11, no. 2, pt. 2 (January).

———. 1964. "Quantitative Aspects of the Economic Growth of Nations: 9, Level and Structure of Foreign Trade: Comparisons for Recent Years." *Economic Development and Cultural Change*, vol. 13, no. 1, pt. 2 (October).

———. 1966. *Modern Economic Growth: Rate, Structure, and Spread*. New Haven, CT: Yale University Press.

———. 1967. "Quantitative Aspects of the Economic Growth of Nations: 10, Level and Structure of Foreign Trade: Long-Term Trends." *Economic Development and Cultural Change*, vol. 15, no. 2, pt. 2 (January).

———. 1971a. *Economic Growth of Nations: Total Output and Production Structure*. Chicago: University of Chicago Press.

———. 1971b. "Modern Economic Growth: Findings and Reflections." Lecture to the Memory of Alfred Nobel, December 11. http://www.nobelprize.org/nobel_prizes/economics/laureates/1971/kuznets-lecture.html (accessed December 30, 2008).

———, ed. 1972. *Quantitative Economic Research: Trends and Problems*. Economic Research: Retrospect and Prospect, Fiftieth Anniversary Colloquia, General Series 96, vol. 7. New York: NBER.

———. 1989. *Economic Development, the Family, and Income Distribution: Selected Essays*. New York: Cambridge University Press.

Lebergott, S. 1964. *Manpower in Economic Growth: The American Record since 1800*. New York: McGraw-Hill.

Lewis, W. A. 1984. "Review: *British Economic Growth*." *Journal of Economic Literature* 22:605–6.

Lewontin, R. C. 1970. "The Units of Selection." *Annual Review of Ecological Systems* 1:1–18.

Li, P. 2009. "China to Outstrip USA in 2009 Auto Sales." China.org.cn, February 11. http://www.china.org.cn/business/2009-02/11/content_17260994.htm (accessed March 29, 2009).

Luce, H. R. 1941. "The American Century." *Life*, February 17, 61–65.

Maddison, A. 1987. "Growth and Slowdown in Advanced Capitalist Economies: Techniques of Quantitative Assessment." *Journal of Economic Literature* 25:649–98.

———. 1991. *Dynamic Forces in Capitalist Development: A Long-Run Comparative View*. Oxford: Oxford University Press.

———. 1995. *Monitoring the World Economy, 1820–1992*. Paris: OECD Development Centre.

———. 1998. *Chinese Economic Performance in the Long Run*. Paris: OECD Development Centre.

———. 2006. *The World Economy*. Paris: OECD Development Centre.

Marshall, A. 1890. *Principles of Economics*. London: Macmillan.

Marx, K. 1904. *A Contribution to the Critique of Political Economy*. Translated by N. Stone. Chicago: Charles H. Kerr.

Matthews, R. C. O., C. H. Feinstein, and J. C. Odling-Smee. 1982. *British Economic Growth, 1856–1973*. Stanford, CA: Stanford University Press.

McLoughlin, W. G. 1978. *Revivals, Awakenings, and Reform: An Essay on Religious Social Change in America, 1607–1977*. Chicago: University of Chicago Press.

Meadows, D. H., D. L. Meadows, J. Randers, and W. W. Behrens III. 1972. *The Limits to Growth: A Report for the Club of Rome's Project on the Predicament of Mankind*. New York: Universe.

Mills, T. C., and N. F. R. Crafts. 2000. "After the Golden Age: A Long-Run Perspective on Growth Rates That Speeded Up, Slowed Down, and Still Differ." *Manchester School* 68:68–91.

Milward, A. S. 1976. "Review: *French Economic Growth*." *International Affairs* 52:642–44.

Mitchell, B. 1947. *Depression Decade: From New Era through New Deal, 1921–1941*. New York: Rinehart.

Mitchell, W. C. 1903. *A History of the Greenbacks with Special Reference to the Economic Consequences of Their Issue: 1862–1865*. Chicago: University of Chicago Press.

———. 1913. *Business Cycles*. Berkeley: University of California Press.

———. 1919. "Statistics and Government." *Publications of the American Statistical Association* 16, no. 125:223.

———. 1937. Preface to *Studies in Income and Wealth* (vol. 1), vii–viii. New York: NBER.

———. 1946. "Empirical Research and the Development of Economic Science." In *Economic Research and the Development of Economic Science and Public Policy*, ed. NBER, 1–20. New York: NBER.

Moran, T. P. 2005. "Kuznets's Inverted U-Curve Hypothesis: The Rise, Demise, and Continued Relevance of a Socioeconomic Law." *Sociological Forum* 20:209–44.

Morrison, W. M. 2006. "China's Economic Conditions." CRS Issue Brief for Congress. Washington, DC: Congressional Research Service, Library of Congress. http://www.fas.org/sgp/crs/row/IB98014.pdf (accessed February 2, 2009).

Myrdal, G. 1968. *Asian Drama: An Inquiry into the Poverty of Nations*. New York: Pantheon.

Nathan, R. 1994. "GNP and Military Mobilization." *Journal of Evolutionary Economics* 4:1–16.

National Bureau of Statistics of China. 2008. *China Statistical Yearbook, 2008*. Beijing: China Statistics Press.

National Intelligence Council (NIC). 2008. *Global Trends, 2025: A Transformed World*. http://www.dni.gov/nic/NIC_2025_project.html (accessed February 3, 2009).

NBER. 1921a. *First Annual Report of the Director of Research to the Board of Directors*. New York: NBER.

———. 1921b. *Income in the United States: Its Amount and Distribution, 1909–1919*. Vol. 1. New York: Harcourt, Brace.

———. 1922a. *Income in the United States: Its Amount and Distribution, 1909–1919*. Vol. 2. New York: Harcourt, Brace.

———. 1922b. *Second Annual Report of the Director of Research to the Board of Directors*. New York: NBER.

———. 1925. *Charter and Bylaws*. New York: NBER.

———. 1931. *Report of the President and Report of the Directors of Research for the Year 1930*. New York: NBER.

———. 1932. *Report of the President and Report of the Directors of Research for the Year 1931*. New York: NBER.

Nearing, S. 1915. *Income: An Examination of the Returns for Services Rendered and from Property Owned in the United States*. New York: Macmillan.

Neihans, J. 1990. *A History of Economic Theory*. Baltimore: Johns Hopkins University Press.

Nelson, R. R., and H. Pack. 1999. "The Asian Miracle and Modern Growth Theory." *Economic Journal* 109, no. 457:416–36.

Nelson, R. R., and S. G. Winter. 1982. *An Evolutionary Theory of Economic Change*. Cambridge: Belknap Press of Harvard University Press.

North, D. C. 1966. *Growth and Welfare in the American Past: A New Economic History*. Englewood Cliffs, NJ: Prentice-Hall.

———. 1968. "Sources of Productivity Change in Ocean Shipping, 1600–1850." *Journal of Political Economy* 76:953–70.

Nunn, N., and N. Quian. 2009. "The Potato's Contribution to Population and Urbanization: Evidence from an Historical Experiment." Working Paper no. w15157. Cambridge, MA: NBER.

OECD. 2005. *Economic Survey of China, 2005*. OECD.org, September 16. http://www.oecd.org/document/12/0,3343,en_2649_34111_35331797_1_1_1,00.html (accessed September 9, 2011).

Ohlin, B. 1971. "Award Ceremony Speech." http://www.nobelprize.org/nobel_prizes/economics/laureates/1971/press.html (accessed September 6, 2011).

Okawa, K., and H. Rosovsky. 1993. *Japanese Economic Growth: Trend Acceleration in the Twentieth Century*. Stanford, CA: Stanford University Press.

Olson, M. 1982. *The Rise and Decline of Nations: Economic Growth, Stagflation, and Social Rigidities*. New Haven, CT: Yale University Press.

Otto, F., H. Gorey, and R. M. Galvin. 1982. "F.D.R.'s Disputed Legacy." *Time*, February 1, 26.

Parrish, J. B. 1967. "Rise of Economics as an Academic Discipline: The Formative Years to 1900." *Southern Economic Journal* 34:1–16.

Patinkin, D. 1976. "Keynes and Econometrics: On the Interaction between Macroeconomic Revolutions of the Interwar Period." *Econometrica* 44:1091–1123.

Pearl, R. 1925. *The Biology of Population Growth*. New York: Norton.

Perkins, D. H. 2006a. "China's Recent Economic Performance and Future Prospects." *Asian Economic Policy Review* 1:15–40.

———. 2006b. "Stagnation and Growth in China over the Millennium: A Comment on Angus Maddison's 'China in the World Economy, 1300–2030.'" *International Journal of Business* 11:255–64.

Potter, Z. L. 1919. "The Central Bureau of Planning and Statistics." *Publications of the American Statistical Association* 16, no. 125:275–85.

Ratner, S. 1967. *Taxation and Democracy in America*. New York: John Wiley.

Rescher, N. 1971. *Temporal Logic*. New York: Springer.

Richardson, G., and P. Van Horn. 2008. "Intensified Regulatory Scrutiny and Bank Distress in New York City during the Great Depression." Working Paper no. w14120. Cambridge, MA: NBER.

Richmond, A., E. Zencey, and C. J. Cleveland. 2007. "Environmental Kuznets Curve." In *Encyclopedia of Earth*, ed. C. J. Cleveland. Washington, DC: Environmental Information Coalition, National Council for Science and the Environment. Available at http://www.eoearth.org/article/Environmental_kuznets_curve.

Ripley, W. Z. 1915. *Railroads: Finance and Organization*. New York: Longmans, Green.

Rockoff, H. 1984. *Drastic Measures: A History of Wage and Price Controls in the United States*. New York: Cambridge University Press.

Rockoff, H., and G. M. Walton. 2005. *History of the American Economy*. 10th ed. Mason, OH: Thomson/South-Western.

Romer, C. 1993. "The Nation in Depression." *Journal of Economic Perspectives* 7, no. 2:19–39.

————. 1999. "Changes in Business Cycles: Evidence and Explanations." *Journal of Economic Perspectives* 13, no. 2:23–44.

Roosevelt, F. D. 1940. "The Great Arsenal of Democracy." Radio broadcast, December 29. Available at http://www.americanrhetoric.com/speeches/fdrarsenalofdemocracy .html.

Rosenberg, N. 1994. "How the Developed Countries Became Rich." *Daedalus* 123, no. 4: 127–40.

Rosovsky, H. 1991. *The University: An Owner's Manual*. New York: Norton.

Rosovsky, H., and K. Okawa. 1973. *Japanese Economic Growth: Trend Acceleration in the Twentieth Century*. London: Oxford University Press.

Rostow, W. W. 1990. *Theorists of Economic Growth: From David Hume to the Present.* New York: Oxford University Press.

Rothbard, M. N. 1972. "War Collectivism in World War I." In *A New History of Leviathan*, ed. R. Radosh and M. N. Rothbard, 66–110. New York: Dutton.

Samuelson, P. A. 1944. "Unemployment Ahead." *New Republic*, September 18, 297–99, 333–35.

Schumpeter, J. A. 1954. *History of Economic Analysis*. Oxford: Oxford University Press.

Schumpeter, J. A., A. H. Cole, and E. S. Mason. 1941. "Frank William Taussig." *Quarterly Journal of Economics* 55, no. 3:353.

Simon, H., and N. Rescher. 1966. "Cause and Counterfactual." *Philosophy of Science* 33:323–40.

Simon, M. 1970. "New British Investment in Canada, 1865–1914." *Canadian Journal of Economics* 3:238–54.

Slicher von Bath, B. H. 1963. *The Agrarian History of Western Europe, AD 500–1850*. London: Edward Arnold.

Smiley, G. 1983. "Recent Unemployment Rate Estimates for the 1920s and 1930s." *Journal of Economic History* 43:487–93.

————. n.d. "Great Depression." *The Concise Encyclopedia of Economics*, ed. David R. Henderson. Library of Economics and Liberty. http://www.econlib.org/library/Enc/ GreatDepression.html (accessed September 9, 2011).

Smith, M. C. 2000. "Mitchell, Wesley Clair." In *American National Biography Online*. http://www.anb.org/articles/14/14-00415.html (accessed May 21, 2009).

Smith, M. K. 1994. *Social Science in the Crucible*. Durham, NC: Duke University Press.

Smith, R. E. 1959. *The Army and Economic Mobilization*. Washington, DC: Office of the Chief of Military History, Department of the Army.

Solow, R. M. 1957. "Technical Change and Aggregate Production Function." *Review of Economics and Statistics* 39:312–20.

Stein, H. 1969. *The Fiscal Revolution in America*. Chicago: University of Chicago Press.

————. 1986. "The Washington Economics Industry." *American Economic Review* 76:1–9.

Stern, D. I. 2004. "The Rise and Fall of the Environmental Kuznets Curve." *World Development* 32:1419–39.

Stigler, G. 1954. "The Early History of Empirical Studies of Consumer Behavior." *Journal of Political Economy* 52:95–113.

Stone, I. 1999. *The Global Export of Capital from Great Britain, 1865–1914: A Statistical Survey*. New York: St. Martin's.

Stone, N. 1916. Review of *Income: An Examination of the Returns for Services Rendered and from Property Owned in the United States*, by S. Nearing. *Intercollegiate Socialist* 4, no. 3:30–35.

Studenski, P. 1958. *The Income of Nations: Theory, Measurement, and Analysis: Past and Present: A Study in Applied Economics and Statistics*. New York: New York University Press.

Summers, L. 2012. "It's Too Soon to Return to Normal Policies." March 25. Available at http://blogs.reuters.com/lawrencesummers/2012/03/26/its-too-soon-to-return-to -normal-policies.

Taussig, F. W. 1882/2009. *The Tariff History of the United States*. Reprint, Ithaca, NY: Cornell University Library.

———. 1911/1939. *Principles of Economics*. 4th ed. New York: Macmillan.

———. 1927. *International Trade*. New York: Macmillan.

Temin, P. 1964. *Iron and Steel in Nineteenth-Century America: An Economic Inquiry*. Cambridge, MA: MIT Press.

Trussell, J., and K. Wachter. 1984. "Estimating Covariates of Height in Truncated Samples." Working Paper no. 1455. Cambridge, MA: NBER.

Tucker, G. 1801. *Letter to a Member of the General Assembly of Virginia on the Subject of the Late Conspiracy of the Slaves with a Proposal for Their Colonization*. Richmond: Printed by H. Pace.

———. 1843. *Progress of the United States in Population and Wealth in Fifty Years, as Exhibited by the Decennial Census*. New York: Little, Brown.

United Nations. Department of Economic and Social Affairs. 1973–78. *The Determinants and Consequences of Population Trends: New Summary of Findings on Interaction of Demographic, Economic and Social Factors*. 2 vols. New York.

"United States Unemployment Rate." n.d. Available at http://www.infoplease.com/ipa/ A0104719.html.

U.S. Bureau of the Census. 1955. *Statistical Abstract of the United States, 1955*. Washington, DC: U.S. Government Printing Office.

———. 1975. *Historical Statistics of the United States: Millennial Edition*. http://www .census.gov/prod/www/abs/statab.html (accessed September 6, 2011).

———. 2003. *Statistical Abstract of the United States, 2003*. Washington, DC: U.S. Government Printing Office.

U.S. Strategic Bombing Survey. 1945. *Summary Report*. Washington, DC: U.S. Government Printing Office.

Wald, A. 1947. *Sequential Analysis*. New York: Wiley.

Warsh, D. 2003. "A Very Short History of the Volunteer Army." *Economic Principles: An Independent Weekly*, July 20. http://www.economicprincipals.com/issues/2003 .07.20/284.html (accessed September 27, 2011).

Wayland, F. 1837. *The Elements of Political Economy*. Boston, Gould, Kendall & Lincoln.

Weiss, T. 1986. "Revised Estimates of the United States Workforce, 1800–1860." In *Long-Term Factors in American Economic Growth*, ed. S. L. Engerman and R. E. Gallman, 641–76. Chicago: University of Chicago Press.

———. 1987. "The Farm Labor Force by Region, 1820–1860: Revised Estimates and Implications for Growth." Working Paper 2438. Cambridge, MA: NBER.

———. 1989. "Economic Growth Before 1860: Revised Conjectures." Historical Working Paper 7. Cambridge, MA: NBER.

White, L. D. 1933. *Trends in Public Administration*. New York: McGraw-Hill.

———. 1937. "New Opportunities for Economists and Statisticians in Federal Employment." *American Economic Review* 27, suppl. 1:210–15.

Wilson, J. Q. 2004. "Sex Matters: Review of *Bare Branches* by Valerie M. Hudson and Andrea M. den Boer." *Wall Street Journal*, July 13.

World Bank. 1993. *The East Asian Miracle: Economic Growth and Public Policy*. New York: Oxford University Press.

Ying, T. 2009. "China February Auto Sales Rise 25% after Tax Cuts." Bloomberg.com, March 10. http://www.bloomberg.com/apps/news?pid=newsarchive&sid=aU3LuPC gYvUo (accessed August 1, 2012).

Young, A. A. 1916. "Nearing's *Income*; King's *Wealth and Income*." *Quarterly Journal of Economics* 30, no. 3:575–87.

Index